GW01604992

THE TAPESTRY ROOM

TWO CHRISTMAS ANGELS.—p. 122.

THE TAPESTRY ROOM

A Child's Romance

By Mrs. MOLESWORTH

'DUDU'

'What tale did Iseult to the children say,
Under the hollies, that bright winter's day?
MATTHEW ARNOLD

ILLUSTRATED BY WALTER CRANE

TOM STACEY

First edition 1879

This edition published 1972 by
Tom Stacey Reprints Ltd.
28-29 Maiden Lane, London WC2E 7JP, England

ISBN 0 85468 230 9

Printed in Great Britain by Biddles Ltd., Guildford, Surrey

LIST OF ILLUSTRATIONS.

CONTENTS.

CHAPTER VIII.

CHAPTER IX.

CHAPTER X.

CHAPTER XI.

CHAPTER XII.

(By Permission.)

TO

H.R.H. VITTORIO EMANUELE

PRINCE OF NAPLES

CROWN PRINCE OF ITALY

ONE OF THE KINDLIEST OF MY YOUNG READERS

MAISON DU CHANOINE,
October 1879.

CHAPTER I.

MADEMOISELLE JEANNE.

"Maitre Corbeau, sur un arbre perché."

LA FONTAINE.

IT was so cold. Ah, so very cold! So thought the old raven as he hobbled up and down the terrace walk at the back of the house—the walk that was so pleasant in summer, with its pretty view of the lower garden, gay with the bright, stiffly-arranged flower-beds, so pleasantly warm and yet shady with the old trees overhead, where the raven's second cousins, the rooks, managed their affairs, not without a good deal of chatter about it, it must be confessed. "Silly creatures," the raven was in the habit of calling them with contempt—all to himself, of course, for no one understood the different tones of his croaking, even though he was a French raven and had received the best of educations. But to-day he was too depressed in spirit by the cold to think of his relations or their behaviour at all. He just hopped or hobbled—I hardly know which you would call it—slowly and solemnly up and down the long walk, where the snow lay so thick that at each hop it came ever so far up his black claws, which annoyed him very much, I assure you, and made him wish more than ever that summer was back again.

Poor old fellow ! he was not usually of a discontented disposition : but to-day, it must be allowed, he was in the right about the cold. It was *very* cold.

Several others beside the raven were thinking so—the three chickens who lived in a queer little house in one corner of the yard thought so, and huddled the closer together, as they settled themselves for the night. For though it was only half-past three in the afternoon, they thought it was no use sitting up any longer on such a make-believe of a day, when not the least little ray of sunshine had succeeded in creeping through the leaden-grey sky. And the tortoise *would* have thought so too if he could, but he was too sleepy to think at all, as he "cruddled" himself into his shell in the corner of the laurel hedge, and dreamt of the nice hot days that were past.

And upstairs, inside the old house, somebody else was thinking so too—a little somebody who seemed to be doing her best to make herself, particularly her nose, colder still, for she was pressing it hard on to the icy window-pane and staring out on to the deserted, snow-covered garden, and thinking how cold it was, and wishing it was summer time again, and fancying how it would feel to be a raven like old "Dudu," all at once, in the mixed-up, dancing-about way that "thinking" was generally done in the funny little brain of Mademoiselle Jeanne.

Inside the room it was getting dark, and the white snow outside seemed to make it darker.

"Mademoiselle Jeanne," said a voice belonging to a servant who just then opened the door; "Mademoiselle Jeanne, what are you doing at the window? You will catch cold."

Jeanne gave a little start when she heard herself spoken to. She had been all alone in the room for some time, with not a sound about her. She turned slowly from the window and came near the fire.

"If I did catch cold, it would not be bad," she said. "I would stay in bed, and you, Marcelline, would make me nice things to eat, and nobody would say, 'Don't do that, Mademoiselle.' It would be charming."

Marcelline was Jeanne's old nurse, and she had been her mother's nurse too. She was really rather old, how old nobody seemed exactly to know, but Jeanne thought her *very* old, and asked her once if she had not been her grandmother's nurse too. Any one else but Marcelline would have been offended at such a question; but Marcelline was not like any one else, and she never was offended at anything. She was so old that for many years no one had seen much difference in her—she had reached a sort of settled oldness, like an arm-chair which may once have been covered with bright-coloured silk, but which, with time and wear, has got to have an all-over-old look which never seems to get any worse Not that Marcelline was dull or grey to look at—she was bright and cheery, and when she had a new clean cap on, all beautifully frilled and crimped round her face, Jeanne used to tell her that she was beautiful, quite beautiful, and that if she was *very* good and always did exactly what Jeanne asked her, she—Jeanne—would have her to be nurse to her children when she had grown up to be a lady, married to some very nice gentleman.

And when Jeanne chattered like that, Marcelline used to smile; she never said anything, she just smiled. Sometimes Jeanne liked to see her smile; sometimes it would make her impatient, and she would say, "Why do you smile like that, Marcelline? *Speak!* When I speak I like you to speak too."

But all she could get Marcelline to answer would be, "Well, Mademoiselle, it is very well what you say."

This evening—or perhaps I should say afternoon, for whatever hour the chickens' timepiece made it, it was only half-past three by the great big clock that stood at the end of the long passage by Jeanne's room door;—this afternoon Jeanne was not quite as lively as she sometimes was. She sat down on the floor in front of the fire and stared into it. It was pretty to look at just then, for the wood was burning redly, and at the tiniest touch a whole bevy of lovely sparks would fly out like bees from a hive, or a covey of birds, or better still, like a thousand imprisoned fairies escaping at some magic touch. Of all things, Jeanne loved to give this magic touch. There was no poker, but she managed just as well with a stick of unburnt wood, or sometimes, when she was *quite* sure Marcelline was not looking, with the toe of her little shoe. Just now it was Marcelline who set the fairy sparks free by moving the logs a little and putting on a fresh one behind.

"How pretty they are, are they not, Marcelline?" said Jeanne.

Marcelline did not speak, and when Jeanne looked up at her, she saw by the light of the fire that she was smiling. Jeanne held up her forefinger.

"Naughty Marcelline," she said; "you are not to smile. You are to *speak.* I want you to speak very much, for it is so dull, and I have nothing to do. I want you to tell me stories, Marcelline. Do you hear, you naughty little thing?"

"And what am I to tell you stories about then, Mademoiselle? You have got all out of my old head long ago; and when the grain is all ground what can the miller do?"

"Get some more, of course," said Jeanne. "Why, *I* could make stories if I tried, I daresay, and I am only seven, and you who are a hundred—are you *quite* a hundred, Marcelline?"

Marcelline shook her head.

"Not *quite*, Mademoiselle," she said.

"Well, never mind, you are old enough to make stories, any way. Tell me more about the country where you lived when you were little as I; the country you will never tell me the name of. Oh, I do like that one about the Golden Princess shut up in the castle by the sea! I like stories about princesses best of all. I do wish I were a princess; next to my best wish of all, I wish to be a princess. Marcelline, do you hear? I want you to tell me a story."

Still Marcelline did not reply. She in her turn was looking into the fire. Suddenly she spoke.

"One, two, three," she said. "Quick, now, Mademoiselle, quick, quick. Wish a wish before that last spark is gone. Quick, Mademoiselle."

"Oh dear, what shall I wish?" exclaimed Jeanne. "When you tell me to be quick it all goes out of my head; but I know now. I wish——"

"Hush, Mademoiselle," said Marcelline, quickly again. "You must not say it aloud. Never mind, it is all right. You have wished it before the spark is gone. It will come true, Mademoiselle."

Jeanne's bright dark eyes glanced up at Marcelline with an expression of mingled curiosity and respect.

"How do you know it will come true?" she said.

Marcelline's old eyes, nearly as bright and dark still as Jeanne's own, had a half-mischievous look in them as she replied, solemnly shaking her head,

"I know, Mademoiselle, and that is all I can say.

And when the time comes for your wish to be granted, you will see if I am not right."

"Shall I?" said Jeanne, half impressed, half rebellious. "Do the fairies tell you things, Marcelline? Not that I believe there are any fairies—not now, any way."

"Don't say that, Mademoiselle," said Marcelline. "In that country I have told you of no one ever said such a thing as that."

"Why didn't they? Did they really *see* fairies there?" asked Jeanne, lowering her voice a little.

"Perhaps," said Marcelline; but that was all she *would* say, and Jeanne couldn't get her to tell her any fairy stories, and had to content herself with making them for herself instead out of the queer shapes of the burning wood of the fire.

She was so busy with these fancies that she did not hear the stopping of the click-click of Marcelline's knitting needles, nor did she hear the old nurse get up from her chair and go out of the room. A few minutes before, the *facteur* had rung at the great wooden gates of the courtyard—a rather rare event, for in those days letters came only twice a week—but this, too, little Jeanne had not heard. She must have grown drowsy with the quiet and the heat of the fire, for she quite started when the door again opened, and Marcelline's voice told her that her mother wanted her to go down to the salon, she had something to say to her.

"O Marcelline," said Jeanne, rubbing her eyes, "I didn't know you had gone away. What does mamma want? O Marcelline, I am so sleepy, I would like to go to bed."

"To go to bed, Mademoiselle, and not yet five o'clock! Oh no, you will wake up nicely by the time you get down to the salon."

"I am so tired, Marcelline," persisted Jeanne. "These winter days it is so dull. I don't mind in summer, for then I can play in the garden with Dudu and the tortoise, and all the creatures. But in winter it is so dull. I would not be tired if I had a little friend to play with me."

"Keep up your heart, Mademoiselle. Stranger things have happened than that you should have some one to play with."

"What do you mean, Marcelline?" said Jeanne, curiously. "Do you know something, Marcelline? Tell me, do. Did you know what my wish was?" she added, eagerly.

"I know, Mademoiselle, that Madame will be

waiting for you in the salon. We can talk about your wish later ; when I am putting you to bed."

She would say no more, but smoothed Jeanne's soft dark hair, never very untidy it must be owned, for it was always neatly plaited in two tails that hung down her back, as was then the fashion for little girls of Jeanne's age and country, and bade her again not to delay going downstairs.

Jeanne set off. In that great rambling old house it was really quite a journey from her room to her mother's salon. There was the long corridor to pass, at one end of which were Jeanne's quarters, at the other a room which had had for her since her babyhood a mingled fascination and awe. It was hung with tapestry, very old, and in some parts faded, but still distinct. As Jeanne passed by the door of this room, she noticed that it was open, and the gleam of the faint moonlight on the snow-covered garden outside attracted her.

"I can see the terrace ever so much better from the tapestry room window," she said to herself. "I wonder what Dudu is doing, poor old fellow. Oh, how cold he must be! I suppose Grignan is asleep in a hole in the hedge, and the chickens will be all right any way. I have not seen Houpet all day."

"Houpet" was Jeanne's favourite of the three chickens. He had come by his name on account of a wonderful tuft of feathers on the top of his head, which stuck straight up and then waved down again, something like a little umbrella. No doubt he was a very rare and wonderful chicken, and if I were clever about chickens I would be able to tell you all his remarkable points. But that I cannot do. I can only say he was the queerest-looking creature that ever pecked about a poultry-yard, and how it came to pass that Jeanne admired him so, I cannot tell you either.

"Poor Houpet!" she repeated, as she ran across the tapestry room to the uncurtained window; "I am sure he must have been very sad without me all day. He has such a loving heart. The others are nice too, but not half so loving. And Grignan has no heart at all; I suppose tortoises never have; only he is very comical, which is nearly as nice. As for Dudu, I really cannot say, he is so stuck up, as if he knew better than any one else. Ah, there he is, the old fellow! Well, Dudu," she called out, as if the raven could have heard her so far off and through the closely shut window; "well, Dudu, how are you today, my dear sir? How do you like the snow and the cold?"

Dudu calmly continued his promenade up and down the terrace. Jeanne could clearly distinguish his black shape against the white ground.

"I am going downstairs to see mamma, Dudu," she went on. "I love mamma very much, but I wish she wasn't my mother at all, but my sister. I wish she was turned into a little girl to play with me, and that papa was turned into a little boy. How funny he would look with his white hair, wouldn't he, Dudu? Oh, you stupid Dudu, why won't you speak to me? I wish you would come up here; there's a beautiful castle and garden in the tapestry, where you would have two peacocks to play with;" for just at that moment the moon, passing from under a cloud, lighted up one side of the tapestry, which, as Jeanne said, represented a garden with various curious occupants. And as the wavering brightness caught the grotesque figures in turn, it really seemed to the little girl as if they moved. Half pleased, half startled at the fancy, she clapped her hands.

"Dudu, Dudu," she cried, "the peacocks want you to come; they're beginning to jump about;" and almost as she said the words a loud croak from the raven sounded in her ears, and turning round, there, to her amazement, she saw Dudu standing on the ledge of the window outside, his bright eyes shining, his black wings flapping, just as if he would say,

"Let me in, Mademoiselle, let me in. Why do you mock me by calling me if you won't let me in?"

Completely startled by this time, Jeanne turned and fled.

"He must be a fairy," she said by herself; "I'll never make fun of Dudu any more—*never*. He must be a fairy, or how else could he have got up from the terrace on to the window-sill all in a minute? And I don't think a raven fairy would be nice at all; he'd be a sort of an imp, I expect. I wouldn't mind now if Houpet was a fairy, he's so gentle and loving; but Dudu would be a sort of ogre fairy, he's so black and solemn. Oh dear, how he startled me! How did he get up there? I'm very glad *I* don't sleep in the tapestry room."

But when she got down to the brightly-lighted salon her cheeks were so pale and her eyes so startled-looking that her mother was quite concerned, and eagerly asked what was the matter.

"Nothing," said Jeanne at first, after the manner of little girls, and boys too, when they do not want to be cross-questioned; but after a while she confessed that she had run into the tapestry room on her way down, and that the moonlight made the figures look as if they were moving—and—and—that Dudu came and stood on the window-sill and croaked at her.

"Dudu stood on the window-sill outside the tapestry room!" repeated her father; "impossible, my child! Why, Dudu could not by any conceivable means get up there; you might as well say you saw the tortoise there too."

"If I had called him perhaps he *would* have come too; I believe Dudu and he are great friends," thought Jeanne to herself, for her mind was in a queer state of confusion, and she would not have felt very much astounded at anything. But aloud she only repeated, "I'm sure he was there, dear papa."

And to satisfy her, her kind father, though he was not so young as he had been, and the bad weather made him very rheumatic, mounted upstairs to the tapestry room, and carefully examined the window inside and out.

"Nothing of the kind to be seen, my little girl," was his report. "Master Dudu was hobbling about in the snow on his favourite terrace walk as usual. I hope the servants give him a little meat in this cold weather, by the by. I must speak to Eugène about it. What you fancied was Dudu, my little Jeanne," he continued, "must have been a branch of the ivy blown across the window. In the moonlight, and with the reflections of the snow, things take queer shapes."

"But there is no wind, and the ivy doesn't grow so high up, and the ivy could not have *croaked*," thought Jeanne to herself again, though she was far too well brought up a little French girl to contradict her father by saying so.

"Perhaps so, dear papa," was all she said.

But her parents still looked a little uneasy.

"She cannot be quite well," said her mother. "She must be feverish. I must tell Marcelline to make her a little tisane when she goes to bed."

"Ah, bah!" said Jeanne's white-headed papa. "What we were speaking of will be a much better cure than tisane. She needs companionship of her own age."

Jeanne pricked up her ears at this, and glanced at her mother inquiringly. Instantly there started into her mind Marcelline's prophecy about her wish.

"The naughty little Marcelline!" she thought to herself. "She has been tricking me. I believe she knew something was going to happen. Mamma, my dear mamma!" she cried, eagerly but respectfully, "have you something to tell me? Have you had letters, mamma, from the country, where the little cousin lives?"

Jeanne's mother softly stroked the cheeks, red enough now, of her excited little daughter.

"Yes, my child," she replied. "I have had a letter. It was for that I sent for you—to tell you about it. I have a letter from the grandfather of Hugh, with whom he has lived since his parents died, and he accepts my invitation. Hugh is to come to live with us, as his mother would have wished. His grandfather can spare him, for he has other grandchildren, and we need him, do we not, my Jeanne? My little girl needs a little brother—and I loved his mother so much," she added in a lower voice.

Jeanne could not speak. Her face was glowing with excitement, her breath came quick and short, almost, it seemed, as if she were going to cry. "O, mamma!" was all she could say—"O mamma!" but her mother understood her.

"And when will he come?" asked Jeanne next.

"Soon, I hope. In a few days; but it depends on the weather greatly. The snow has stopped the diligences in several places, they say; but his grandfather writes that he would like Hugh to come soon, as he himself has to leave home."

"And will he be always with us? Will he do lessons with me, mamma, and go to the château with us in summer, and always be with us?"

"I hope so. For a long time at least. And he will do lessons with you at first—though when he gets big he will need more teachers, of course."

"He is a year older than I, mamma."

"Yes, he is eight."

"And, mamma," added Jeanne, after some consideration, "what room will he have?"

"The tapestry room," said her mother. "It is the warmest, and Hugh is rather delicate, and may feel it cold here. And the tapestry room is not far from yours, my little Jeanne, so you can keep your toys and books together. There is only one thing I do not quite understand in the letter," went on Jeanne's mother, turning to her husband as she always did in any difficulty—he was so much older and wiser than she, she used to say. "Hugh's grandfather says Hugh has begged leave to bring a pet with him, and he hopes I will not mind. What can it be? I cannot read the other word."

"A little dog probably," said Jeanne's father, putting on his spectacles as he took the letter from his wife, "a pet—gu—ga—and then comes another word beginning with 'p.' It almost looks like 'pig,' but it could not be a pet pig. No, I cannot read it either; we must wait to see till he comes."

As Marcelline was preparing to put Jeanne to bed that night, the little girl suddenly put her arms round her nurse's neck, and drew down her old face till it was on a level with her own.

"Look in my face, Marcelline," she said. "Now look in my face and confess. Now, didn't you know that mamma had got a letter to-night and what it said, and was not that how you knew my wish would come true?"

Marcelline smiled.

"That was one way I knew, Mademoiselle," she said.

"Well, it shows I'm right not to believe in fairies any way. I really did think at first that the fairies had told you something, but——" suddenly she stopped as the remembrance of her adventure in the tapestry room returned to her mind. "Dudu may be a fairy, whether Marcelline has anything to do with fairies or not," she reflected. It was better certainly to approach such subjects respectfully. "Marcelline," she added, after a little silence, "there is only one thing

I don't like. I wish the little cousin were not going to sleep in the tapestry room."

"Not in the tapestry room, Mademoiselle?" exclaimed Marcelline, "why, it is the best room in the house! You, who are so fond of stories, Mademoiselle —why there are stories without end on the walls of the tapestry room; particularly on a moonlight night."

"*Are* there?" said Jeanne. "I wonder then if the little cousin will be able to find them out. If he does, he must tell them to me. Are they fairy stories, Marcelline?"

But old Marcelline only smiled.

CHAPTER II.

PRINCE CHÉRI.

"I'll take my guinea-pig always to church."

CHILD WORLD.

IF it were cold just then in the thick-walled, well-warmed old house, which was Jeanne's home, you may fancy *how* cold it was in the rumbling diligence, which in those days was the only way of travelling in France. And for a little boy whose experience of long journeys was small, this one was really rather trying. But Jeanne's cousin Hugh was a very patient little boy. His life, since his parents' death, had not been a *very* happy one, and he had learnt to bear troubles without complaining. And now that he was on his way to the kind cousins his mother had so often told him of, the cousins who had been so kind to *her*, before she had any home of her own, his heart was so full of happiness that, even if the journey had been twice as cold and uncomfortable, he would not have thought himself to be pitied.

It was a pale little face, however, which looked

out of the diligence window at the different places where it stopped, and a rather timid voice which asked in the pretty broken French he had not quite forgotten since the days that his mother taught him her own language, for a little milk for his "pet." The pet, which had travelled on his knees all the way from England—comfortably nestled up in hay and cotton wool in its cage, which looked something like a big mouse-trap—much better off in its way certainly than its poor little master. But it was a great comfort to him: the sight of its funny little nose poking out between the bars of its cage made Hugh feel ever so much less lonely, and when he had secured a little milk for his guinea-pig he did not seem to mind half so much about anything for himself.

Still it was a long and weary journey, and poor Hugh felt very glad when he was wakened up from the uncomfortable dose, which was all in the way of sleep he could manage, to be told that at last they had arrived. This was the town where his friends lived, and a "monsieur," the conductor added, was inquiring for him—Jeanne's father's valet it was, who had been sent to meet him and take him safe to the old house, where an eager little heart was counting the minutes till he came.

They looked at each other curiously when at last they met. Jeanne's eyes were sparkling and her cheeks burning, and her whole little person in a flutter of joyful excitement, and yet she couldn't speak. Now that the little cousin was there, actually standing before her, she could not speak. How was it? He was not *quite* what she had expected; he looked paler and quieter than any boys she had seen, and—was he not glad to see her?—glad to have come? —she asked herself with a little misgiving. She looked at him again—his blue eyes were very sweet and gentle, and, tired though he was, Jeanne could see that he was trying to smile and look pleased. But he was *very* tired and very shy. That was all that was the matter. And his shyness made Jeanne feel shy too.

"Are you very tired, my cousin?" she said at last.

"Not very, thank you," said Hugh. "I am rather tired, but I am not very hungry," he added, glancing at a side-table where a little supper had been laid out for him. "I am not very hungry, but I think Nibble is. Might I have a little milk for Nibble, please?"

As he spoke he held up for Jeanne to see the small box he was carrying, and she gave a little scream of pleasure when, through the bars, she caught sight of the guinea-pig's soft nose, poking out, saying as plainly almost as if he had spoken, "I want my supper; please to see at once about my supper, little girl."

"Neeble," cried Jeanne, "O my cousin, is Neeble your pet? Why, he is a 'cochon de Barbarie!' O the dear little fellow! We could not—at least papa and mamma could not—read what he was. And have you brought him all the way, my cousin, and do you love him very much? Marcelline, Marcelline, oh, do give us some milk for the cochon de Barbarie—oh, see, Marcelline, how sweet he is!"

Once set free, her tongue ran on so fast that sometimes Hugh had difficulty to understand her. But the ice was broken any way, and when, an hour or two later, Jeanne's mother told her she might take Hugh up to show him his room, the two trotted off, hand-in-hand, as if they had been close companions for years.

"I hope you will like your room, chéri," said Jeanne, with a tiny tone of patronising. "It is not very far from mine, and mamma says we can keep all our toys and books together in my big cupboard in the passage."

Hugh looked at Jeanne for a moment without speaking. "What was that name you called me just now, Jeanne?" he asked, after a little pause.

Jeanne thought for a minute.

"'Mon cousin,' was it that?" she said. "Oh no, I remember, it was 'chéri.' I *cannot* say your name—I have tried all these days. I cannot say it better than 'Ee-ou,' which is not pretty."

She screwed her rosy little mouth into the funniest shape as she tried to manage "Hugh." Hugh could hardly help laughing.

"Never mind," he said. "I like 'chéri' ever so much better. I like it better than 'mon cousin' or any name, because, do you know," he added, dropping his voice a little, "I remember now, though I had forgotten till you said it—that was the name mamma called me by."

"Chéri!" repeated Jeanne, stopping half-way up the staircase to throw her arms round Hugh's neck at the greatest risk to the equilibrium of the whole party, including the guinea-pig—"*Chéri*! I shall always call you so, then. You shall be my Prince Chéri. Don't you love fairy stories, mon cousin?"

"*Awfully*," said Hugh, from the bottom of his soul.

"I knew you would," said Jeanne triumphantly. "And oh, so do I! Marcelline says, Chéri, that the tapestry room—that's the room you're going to have

—is full of fairy stories. I wonder if you'll find out any of them. You must tell me if you do."

"The tapestry room?" repeated Hugh; "I don't think I ever saw a tapestry room. Oh," he added, as a sudden recollection struck him, "is it like what that queen long ago worked about the battles and all that? I mean all about William the Conqueror."

"No," said Jeanne, "it's quite different from that work. I've seen that, so I know. It isn't pretty at all. It's just long strips of linen with queer-shaped horses and things worked on. Not *at all* pretty. And I think the pictures on the walls of your room *are* pretty. Here it is. Isn't it a funny room, Chéri?"

She opened the door of the tapestry room as she spoke, for while chattering they had mounted the staircase and made their way along the corridor. Hugh followed his little cousin into the room, and stood gazing round him with curious surprise and pleasure. The walls were well lighted up, for Marcelline had carried a lamp upstairs and set it down on the table, and a bright fire was burning in the wide old-fashioned hearth.

"Jeanne," said Hugh, after a minute's silence, "Jeanne, it is very funny, but, do you know, I am *sure* I have seen this room before. I seem to know the pictures on the walls. Oh, *how* nice they are! I didn't think that was what tapestry meant. Oh, how glad I am this is to be my room—is yours like this too, Jeanne?"

Jeanne shook her head.

"Oh no, Chéri," she said. "My room has a nice paper—roses and things like that running up and down. I am very glad my room is not like this. I don't think I should like to see all these funny creatures in the night. You don't know how queer they look in the moonlight. They quite frightened me once."

Hugh opened his blue eyes very wide.

"*Frightened* you?" he said. "I should never be frightened at them. They are so nice and funny. Just look at those peacocks, Jeanne. They are lovely."

Jeanne still shook her head.

"I don't think so," she said. "I can't bear those peacocks. But I'm very glad *you* like them, Chéri."

"I wish it was moonlight to-night," continued Hugh. "I don't think I should go to sleep at all. I would lie awake watching all the pictures. I dare say they look rather nice in the firelight too, but still not *so* nice as in the moonlight."

"No, Monsieur," said Marcelline, who had followed the children into the room. "A moonlight night is the time to see them best. It makes the colours look quite fresh again. Mademoiselle Jeanne has never looked at the tapestry properly by moonlight, or she would like it better."

"I shouldn't mind with Chéri," said Jeanne. "You must call me some night when it's very pretty, Chéri, and we'll look at it together."

Marcelline smiled and seemed pleased, which was rather funny. Most nurses would have begun scolding Jeanne for dreaming of such a thing as running about the house in the middle of the night to admire the moonlight on tapestry or on anything else. But then Marcelline certainly was rather a funny person.

"And the cochon de Barbarie, where is he to sleep, Monsieur?" she said to Hugh.

Hugh looked rather distressed.

"I don't know," he said. "At home he slept in his little house on a sort of balcony there was outside my window. But there isn't any balcony here—besides, it's so *very* cold, and he's quite strange, you know."

He looked at Marcelline, appealingly.

"I daresay, while it is so cold, Madame would not

mind if we put him in the cupboard in the passage," she said; but Jeanne interrupted her.

"Oh no," she said. "He would be far better in the chickens' house. It's nice and warm, I know, and his cage can be in one corner. He wouldn't be nearly so lonely, and to-morrow I'll tell Houpet and the others that they must be very kind to him. Houpet always does what I tell him."

"Who is Houpet?" said Hugh.

"He's my pet chicken," replied Jeanne. "They're all pets, of course, but he's the most of a pet of all. He lives in the chicken-house with the two other little chickens. O Chéri," she added, glancing round, and seeing that Marcelline had left the room, "do let us run out and peep at Houpet for a minute. We can go through the tonnelle, and the chickens' house is close by."

She darted off as she spoke, and Hugh, nothing loth, his precious Nibble still in his arms, followed her. They ran down the long corridor, on to which opened both the tapestry room and Jeanne's room at the other end, through a small sort of anteroom, and then—for though they were *upstairs*, the garden being built in terraces was at this part of the house on a level with the first floor—then straight out into what little Jeanne called "the tonnelle."

Hugh stood still and gazed about him with delight and astonishment.

"O Jeanne," he exclaimed, "how pretty it is! oh, how very pretty!"

Jeanne stopped short in her progress along the tonnelle.

"What's pretty?" she said in a matter-of-fact tone. "Do you mean the garden with the snow?"

"No, no, that's pretty too, but I mean the trees. Look up, Jeanne, do."

There was no moonlight, but the light from the windows streamed out to where the children stood, and shone upon the beautiful icicles on the branches above their heads. For the tonnelle was a kind of arbour—a long covered passage made by trees at each side, whose boughs had been trained to meet and interlace overhead. And now, with their fairy tracery of snow and frost, the effect of the numberless little branches forming a sparkling roof was pretty and fanciful in the extreme. Jeanne looked up as she was told.

"Yes," she said, "it's pretty. If it was moonlight it would be prettier still, for then we could see right along the tonnelle to the end."

"I don't think that *would* be prettier," said Hugh;

"the dark at the end makes it look so nice—like as if it was a fairy door into some queer place—a magic cavern, or some place like that."

"So it does," said Jeanne. "What nice fancies you have, Chéri! But I wish you could see the tonnelle in summer. It *is* pretty then, with all the leaves on. But we must run quick, or else Marcelline will be calling us before we have got to the chicken-house."

Off she set again, and Hugh after her, though not so fast, for Jeanne knew every step of the way, and poor Hugh had never been in the garden before. It was not very far to go, however—the chickens' house was in a little courtyard just a few steps from the tonnelle, and guided by Jeanne's voice in front as much as by the faint glimpses of her figure, dark against the snow, Hugh soon found himself safe beside her at the door of the chickens' house. Jeanne felt about till she got hold of the latch, which she lifted, and was going to push open the door and enter when Hugh stopped her.

"Jeanne," he said, "it's *quite* dark. We can't possibly see the chickens. Hadn't we better wait till to-morrow, and put Nibble in the cupboard, as Marcelline said, for to-night?"

"Oh no," said Jeanne. "It doesn't matter a bit that it's dark." She opened the door as she spoke, and gently pulled Hugh in after her. "Look," she went on, "there is a very, very little light from the kitchen window after all, when the door is opened. Look, Chéri, up in that corner sleep Houpet and the others. Put the cochon de Barbarie down here—so—that will do. He will be quite safe here, and you feel it is not cold."

"And are there no rats, or naughty dogs about—nothing like that?" asked Hugh rather anxiously.

"Of course not," replied Jeanne. "Do you think I'd leave Houpet here if there were? I'll call to Houpet now, and tell him to be kind to the little cochon."

"But Houpet's asleep, and, besides, how would he know what you say?" objected Hugh.

For all answer Jeanne gave a sort of little whistle—half whistle, half coo it was. "Houpet, Houpet," she called softly, "we've brought a little cochon de Barbarie to sleep in your house. You must be very kind to him—do you hear, Houpet dear? and in the morning you must fly down and peep in at his cage and tell him you're very glad to see him."

A faint, a very faint little rustle was heard up

above in the corner where Jeanne had tried to persuade her cousin that the chickens were to be *seen*, and delighted at this evidence that any way they were to be *heard*, she turned to him triumphantly.

"That's Houpet," she said. "Dear little fellow, he's too sleepy to crow—he just gives a little wriggle to show that he's heard me. Now put down the cage, Chéri—oh, you have put it down—and let's run in again. Your pet will be quite safe, you see, but if we're not quick, Marcelline will be running out to look for us."

She felt about for Hugh's hand, and having got it, turned to go. But she stopped to put her head in again for a moment at the door.

"Houpet, dear," she said, "don't let Dudu come into your house. If he tries to, you must fly at him and scold him and peck him."

"Who is Dudu?" said Hugh, as they were running back to the house together along the snowy garden path.

"He is——" began Jeanne. "Hush," she went on, in a lower voice, "there he is! I do believe he heard what I said, and he's angry." For right before them on the path stood the old raven, on one leg as usual, though this it was too dark to see clearly.

And, as Jeanne spoke, he gave a sharp, sudden croak, which made both the children jump, and then deliberately hopped away.

"He's a raven!" said Hugh with surprise. "Why, what funny pets you have, Jeanne!"

Jeanne laughed.

"Dudu isn't my pet," she said. "I don't like him. To tell you the truth, Chéri, I'm rather frightened of him. I think he's a sort of a fairy."

Hugh looked much impressed, but not at all surprised.

"Do you really, Jeanne?" he said.

"Yes," she said, "I do. And I'm not *sure* but that Grignan is too. At least I think Grignan is enchanted, and that Dudu is the spiteful fairy that did it. Grignan is the tortoise, you know."

"Yes," said Hugh, "you told me about him. I do wonder if what you think is true," he added reflectively. "We must try to find out, Jeanne."

"But we mustn't offend Dudu," said Jeanne. "He might, you know, turn *us* into something—two little mice, perhaps—that wouldn't be very nice, would it, Chéri?"

"I don't know," Hugh replied. "I wouldn't mind for a little, if he would turn us back again. We could get into such funny places and see such funny things—couldn't we, Jeanne?"

They both laughed merrily at the idea, and were still laughing when they ran against Marcelline at the door which they had left open at the end of the tonnelle.

"My children!" she exclaimed. "Monsieur Chéri and Mademoiselle Jeanne! Where have you been? And in the snow too! Who would have thought it?"

Her tone was anxious, but not cross. She hurried them in to the warm fire, however, and carefully examined their feet to make sure that their shoes and stockings were not wet.

"Marcelline is very kind," said Hugh, fixing his soft blue eyes on the old nurse in surprise. "At home, grandmamma's maid would have scolded me dreadfully if I had run out in the snow."

"Yes," said Jeanne, flinging her arms round the old nurse's neck, and giving her a kiss first on one cheek then on the other; "she is very kind. Nice little old Marcelline."

"Perhaps," said Hugh, meditatively, "she remembers that when she was a little girl she liked to do things like that herself."

"I don't believe you ever were a little girl, were

you, Marcelline?" said Jeanne. "I believe you were always a little old woman like what you are now."

Marcelline laughed, but did not speak.

"Ask Dudu," she said at last. "If he is a fairy, he should know."

Jeanne pricked up her ears at this.

"Marcelline," she said solemnly, "I believe you do know something about Dudu. Oh, *do* tell us, dear Marcelline."

But nothing more was to be got out of the old nurse.

When the children were undressed, Jeanne begged leave to run into Hugh's room with him to tuck him into bed, and make him feel at home the first night. There was no lamp in the room, but the firelight danced curiously on the quaint figures on the walls.

"You're sure you're not frightened, Chéri?" said little Jeanne in a motherly way, as she was leaving the room.

"Frightened! what is there to be frightened at?" said Hugh.

"The funny figures," said Jeanne. "Those peacocks look just as if they were going to jump out at you."

"I think they look very nice," said Hugh. "I am

sure I shall have nice dreams. I shall make the peacocks give a party some night, Jeanne, and we'll invite Dudu and Grignan, and Houpet and the two little hens, and Nibble, of course, and we'll make them all tell stories."

Jeanne clapped her hands.

"Oh, what fun!" she exclaimed. "And you'll ask me and let me hear the stories, won't you, Chéri?"

"*Of course,*" said Hugh. So Jeanne skipped off in the highest spirits.

CHAPTER III.

ON A MOONLIGHT NIGHT.

"O moon! in the night I have seen you sailing,
And shining so round and low."

CHILD NATURE.

"AND what did you dream, Chéri?" inquired Jeanne the next morning in a confidential and mysterious tone.

Hugh hesitated.

"I don't know," he said at last. "At least——" he stopped and hesitated again.

The two children were having their "little breakfast," consisting of two great big cups of nice hot milky coffee and two big slices of bread, with the sweet fresh butter for which the country where Jeanne's home was is famed. They were alone in Jeanne's room, and Marcelline had drawn a little table close to the fire for them, for this morning it seemed colder than ever; fresh snow had fallen during the night, and out in the garden nothing was to be seen but smoothly-rounded white mounds of varying sizes and heights, and up in the sky the dull blue-grey curtain of snow-cloud made one draw back shivering from the window, feeling as if the sun had gone off in a sulky fit and would *never* come back again.

But inside, close by the brightly-blazing wood fire, Jeanne and Hugh found themselves "very well," as the little girl called it, very well indeed. And the hot coffee was very nice, much nicer, Hugh thought, than the very weak tea which his grandmother's maid used to give him for breakfast at home. He stirred it round and round slowly with his spoon, staring into his cup, while he repeated, in answer to little Jeanne's question about what he had dreamt, "No, I don't know."

"But you did dream *something*," said Jeanne rather impatiently. "Can't you tell me about it? I thought you were going to have all sorts of funny things to tell me. You said you would have a party of the peacocks and all the pets, and make them tell stories."

"Yes," said Hugh slowly. "But I couldn't make them—I must wait till they come. I think I did dream some funny things last night, but I can't remember. There seemed to be a lot of chattering, and once I thought I saw the raven standing at the end of the bed, but that time I wasn't dreaming. I'm sure I wasn't; but I was very sleepy, and I couldn't hear what he said. He seemed to want me to do something or other, and then he nodded his head to where the peacocks are, and do you know, Jeanne, I thought they nodded too. Wasn't that funny? But I daresay it was only the firelight—the fire had burnt low, and then it bobbed up again all of a sudden."

"And what more?" asked Jeanne eagerly. "O Chéri, I think that's wonderful! Do tell me some more."

"I don't think I remember any more," said Hugh. "After that I went to sleep, and then it was all a muddle. There were the chickens and Nibble and the tortoise all running about, and Dudu seemed to be talking to me all the time. But it was just a muddle; you know how dreams go sometimes. And when I woke up the fire was quite out and it was all dark. And then I saw the light of Marcelline's candle through the hinge of the door, and she came to tell me it was time to get up."

"Oh dear," said Jeanne, "I do hope you'll dream some more to-night."

"I daresay I shan't dream at all," said Hugh. "Some nights I go to sleep, and it's morning in one minute. I don't like that much, because it's nice to wake up and feel how cosy it is in bed."

"But, Chéri," pursued Jeanne after a few moments' silence, and a few more bites at her bread and butter, "there's one thing I don't understand. It's about Dudu. You said it wasn't a dream, you were sure. Do you think he was really there, at the foot of the bed? It might have been the firelight that made you think you saw the peacocks nodding, but it couldn't have been the firelight that made you think you saw Dudu."

"No," said Hugh, "I can't understand it either. If it was a dream it was a very queer one, for I never felt more awake in my life. I'll tell you what, Jeanne, the next time I think I see Dudu like that I'll run and tell you."

"Yes, do," said Jeanne, "though I don't know that it would be much good. Dudu's dreadfully tricky."

She had not told Hugh of the trick the raven had played her, though why she had not done so she could hardly have explained. Perhaps she was a little ashamed of having been so frightened; perhaps she was still a little afraid of Dudu; and most of all.

I think, she had a great curiosity to find out more about the mysterious bird, and thought it best to leave Hugh to face his own adventures.

"If Dudu thinks I've told Chéri all about his funny ways," she thought, "perhaps he'll be angry and not do any more queer things."

The snow was still, as I said, thick on the ground, thicker, indeed, than the day before. But the children managed to amuse themselves very well. Marcelline would not hear of their going out, not even as far as the chickens' house, but she fetched Nibble to pay them a visit in the afternoon, and they had great fun with him.

"He looks very happy, doesn't he, Chéri?" said Jeanne. "I am sure Houpet has been kind to him. What a pity pets can't speak, isn't it? they could tell us such nice funny things."

"Yes," said Hugh, "I've often thought that, and I often have thought Nibble could speak if he liked."

"*Houpet* could, I'm quite sure," said Jeanne, "and I believe Dudu and he do speak to each other. You should just see them sometimes. Why, there they are!" she added, going close up to the window near which she had been standing. "Do come here, Chéri, quick, but come very quietly."

Hugh came forward and looked out. There were the four birds, making the quaintest group you could fancy. Houpet with his waving tuft of feathers was perched on the top rung of a short garden ladder, his two little hens as usual close beside him. And down below on the path stood the raven, on one leg of course, his queer black head very much on one side, as he surveyed the little group above him.

"Silly young people," he seemed to be saying to himself; but Houpet was not to be put down so. With a shrill, clear crow he descended from his perch, stepped close up to Dudu, looked him in the face, and then quietly marched off, followed by his two companions. The children watched this little scene with the greatest interest.

"They *do* look as if they were talking to each other," said Hugh. "I wonder what it's about."

"Perhaps it's about the party," said Jeanne; "the party you said you'd give to the peacocks on the wall, and all the pets."

"Perhaps," said Hugh. "I am sure there must be beautiful big rooms in that castle with the lots of steps up to it, where the peacocks stand. Don't you think it would be nice to get inside that castle and see what it's like?"

"Oh, wouldn't it!" said Jeanne, clapping her hands. "How I do wish we could! You might tell Dudu to take us, Chéri. Perhaps it's a fairy palace really, though it only looks like a picture, and if Dudu's a fairy, he might know about it."

"I'll ask him if I get a chance," said Hugh. "Good morning, Monsieur Dudu," he went on, bowing politely from the window to the raven, who had cocked his head in another direction, and seemed now to be looking up at the two children with the same supercilious stare he had bestowed upon the cock and hens. "Good morning, Monsieur Dudu; I hope you won't catch cold with this snowy weather. It's best to be very polite to him, you see," added Hugh, turning to Jeanne; "for if he took offence we should get no fun out of him."

"Oh yes," said Jeanne, "it is much best to be very polite to him. Look at him now, Chéri; *doesn't* he look as if he knew what we were saying?"

For Dudu was eyeing them unmistakably by this time, his head more on one side than ever, and his lame leg stuck out in the air like a walking-stick.

"That's *just* how he stood at the foot of the bed, on the wood part, you know," said Hugh, in a whisper.

"And weren't you frightened, Chéri?" said Jeanne. "I always think Dudu looks not at all like a good fairy, when he cocks his head on one side and sticks his claw out like that. I quite believe then that he's a wicked enchanter. O Chéri," she went on, catching hold of Hugh, "what *should* we do if he was to turn us into two little frogs or toads?"

"We should have to live in the water, and eat nasty little worms and flies, I suppose," said Hugh gravely.

"And that sort of thick green stuff that grows at the top of dirty ponds; fancy having that for soup," said Jeanne pathetically. "O Chéri, we must indeed be very polite to Dudu, and take *great* pains not to offend him; and if he comes to you in the night, you must be sure to call me at once."

But the following night and several nights after that went by, and nothing was heard or seen of Monsieur Dudu. The weather got a little milder; that is to say, the snow gradually melted away, and the children were allowed to go out into the garden and visit their pets. Nibble seemed quite at home in his new quarters, and was now permitted to run about the chicken-house at his own sweet will; and Jeanne greatly commended Houpet for his kindness to the little stranger, which commendation the chicken received in very good part, particularly when it took the shape of all the tit-bits left on the children's plates.

"See how tame he is," said Jeanne one day when she had persuaded the little cock to peck some crumbs out of her hand; "isn't he a darling, Chéri, with his *dear* little tuft of feathers on the top of his head?"

"He's awfully funny-looking," said Hugh, consideringly; "do you really think he's very pretty, Jeanne?"

"Of course I do," said Jeanne, indignantly; "all my pets are pretty, but Houpet's the prettiest of all."

"He's prettier than Grignan, certainly," said Hugh, giving an amiable little push to the tortoise, who happened to be lying at his feet; "but I like Grignan, he's so comical."

"I think Grignan must know a great deal," said Jeanne, "he's so solemn."

"So is Dudu," said Hugh. "By the by, Jeanne," he went on, but stopped suddenly.

"What?" said Jeanne.

"It just came into my head while we were talking

that I must have dreamt of Dudu again last night; but now I try to remember it, it has all gone out of my head."

"*What* a pity," said Jeanne; "do try to remember. Was it that he came and stood at the foot of the bed again, like the last time? You promised to call me if he did."

"No, I don't think he did. I have more a sort of feeling that he and the peacocks on the wall were whispering to each other—something about us—you and me, Jeanne—it was, I think."

"Perhaps they were going to give a party, and were planning about inviting us," suggested Jeanne.

"I don't know," said Hugh; "it's no good my trying to think. It's just a sleepy feeling of having heard something. I can't remember anything else, and the more I think, the less I remember."

"Well, you must be sure to tell me if you do hear anything more. I was awake ever so long in the night, ever so long; but I didn't mind, there was such nice moonlight."

"Moonlight, was there?" said Hugh; "I didn't know that. I'll try to keep awake to-night, because Marcelline says the figures on the walls are so pretty when it's moonlight."

"And if Dudu comes, or you see anything funny, you'll promise to call me?" said Jeanne.

Hugh nodded his head. There was not much fear of his forgetting his promise. Jeanne reminded him of it at intervals all that day, and when the children kissed each other for good-night she whispered again, "Remember to call me, Chéri."

Chéri went to sleep with the best possible intentions as to "remembering." He had, first of all, intended not to go to sleep at all, for his last glance out of the window before going to bed showed him Monsieur Dudu on the terrace path, enjoying the moonlight apparently, but, Hugh strongly suspected, bent on mischief, for his head was very much on one side and his claw very much stuck out, in the way which Jeanne declared made him look like a very impish raven indeed.

"I wonder what Marcelline meant about the moonlight," thought Hugh to himself as he lay down. "I hardly see the figures on the wall at all. The moon must be going behind a cloud. I wonder if it will be brighter in the middle of the night. I don't see that I need stay awake all the night to see. I can easily wake again. I'll just take a little sleep first."

And the little sleep turned out such a long one,

that when poor Hugh opened his eyes, lo and behold! it was to-morrow morning—there was Marcelline standing beside the bed, telling him it was time to get up, he would be late for his tutor if he did not dress himself at once.

"Oh dear," exclaimed Hugh, "what a pity! I meant to stay awake all night to watch the moonlight."

Marcelline smiled what Jeanne called her funny smile.

"You would find it very difficult to do that, I think, my little Monsieur," she said. "However, you did not miss much last night. The clouds came over so that the moon had no chance. Perhaps it will be clearer to-night."

With this hope Hugh had to be satisfied, and to satisfy also his little cousin, who was at first quite disappointed that he had nothing wonderful to tell her.

"To-night," she said, "*I* shall stay awake all night, and if the moonlight is very nice and bright I shall come and wake *you*, you sleepy Chéri. I do *so* want to go up those steps and into the castle where the peacocks are standing at the door."

"So do I," said Hugh, rather mortified; "but if

one goes to sleep, whose fault is it? I am sure you will go to sleep too, if you try to keep awake. There's *nothing* makes people go to sleep so fast as trying to keep awake."

"Well, don't try then," said Jeanne, "and see what comes then."

And when night came, Hugh, partly perhaps because he was particularly sleepy—the day had been so much finer that the children had had some splendid runs up and down the long terrace walk in the garden, and the unusual exercise had made both of them very ready for bed when the time came—took Jeanne's advice, tucked himself up snugly and went off to sleep without thinking of the moonlight, or the peacocks, or Dudu, or anything. He slept so soundly, that when he awoke he thought it was morning, and brighter morning than had hitherto greeted him since he came to Jeanne's home.

"Dear me!" he said to himself, rubbing his eyes, "it must be very late; it looks just as if summer had come," for the whole room was flooded with light—such beautiful light—bright and clear, and yet soft. No wonder that Hugh rubbed his eyes in bewilderment—it was not till he sat up in bed and looked well about him, quite awake now, that he saw that after all it was moonlight, not sunshine, which was illumining the old tapestry room and everything which it contained in this wonderful way.

"Oh, how pretty it is!" thought Hugh. "No wonder Marcelline told us that we should see the tapestry in the moonlight. I never could have thought it would have looked so pretty. Why, even the peacocks' tails seem to have got all sorts of new colours."

He leant forward to examine them better. They were standing—just as usual—one on each side of the flight of steps leading up to the castle. But as Hugh gazed at them it certainly seemed to him—could it be his fancy only?—no, it *must* be true—that their long tails grew longer and swept the ground more majestically—then that suddenly—fluff! a sort of little wind seemed to rustle for an instant, and fluff! again, the two peacocks had spread their tails, and now stood with them proudly reared fan-like, at their backs, just like the real living birds that Hugh had often admired in his grandfather's garden. Hugh was too much amazed to rub his eyes again—he could do nothing but stare, and stare he did with all his might, but for a moment or two there was nothing else to be seen. The pea-

IT WAS DUDU!—p. 51.

cocks stood still—so still that Hugh now began to doubt whether they had not always stood, tails spread, just as he saw them now, and whether these same tails having ever drooped on the ground was not altogether his fancy. A good deal puzzled, and a little disappointed, he was turning away to look at another part of the pictured walls, when again a slight flutter of movement caught his eyes. What was about to happen this time?

"Perhaps they are going to furl their tails again," thought Hugh; but no. One on each side of the castle door, the peacocks solemnly advanced a few steps, then stood still—quite still—but yet with a certain waiting look about them as if they were expecting some one or something. They were not kept waiting long. The door of the castle opened slowly, very slowly, the peacocks stepped still a little farther forward, and out of the door of the castle—the castle into which little Jeanne had so longed to enter—who, what, who *do* you think came forth? It was Dudu!

A small black figure, black from head to foot, head very much cocked on one side, foot—claw I should say—stuck out like a walking-stick; he stood between the peacocks, right in Hugh's view, just in front of the door which had closed behind him, at the top of the high flight of steps. He stood still with an air of great dignity, which seemed to say, "Here you see me for the first time in my rightful character—monarch of all I survey." And somehow Hugh felt that this unspoken address was directed to *him*. Then, quietly and dignifiedly still, the raven turned, first to the right, then to the left, and gravely bowed to the two attendant peacocks, who each in turn saluted him respectfully and withdrew a little farther back, on which Dudu began a very slow and imposing progress down the steps. How he succeeded in making it so imposing was the puzzle, for after all, his descent was undoubtedly a series of hops, but all the same it was very majestic, and Hugh felt greatly impressed, and watched him with bated breath.

"One, two, three, four," said Hugh to himself, half unconsciously counting each step as the raven advanced, "what a lot of steps! Five, six, seven," up to twenty-three Hugh counted on. And "what is he going to do now?" he added, as Dudu, arrived at the foot of the stairs, looked calmly about him for a minute or two, as if considering his next movements. Then—how he managed it Hugh could not tell—he suddenly stepped out of the tapestry landscape, and in another moment was perched in his old place at the foot of Hugh's bed.

He looked at Hugh for an instant or two, gravely and scrutinisingly, then bowed politely. Hugh, who was half sitting up in bed, bowed too, but without speaking. He remembered Jeanne's charges to be very polite to the raven, and thought it better to take no liberties with him, but to wait patiently till he heard what Monsieur Dudu had to say. For somehow it seemed to him a matter of course that the raven *could* speak—he was not the very least surprised when at last Dudu cleared his throat pompously and began—

"You have been expecting me, have you not?"

Hugh hesitated.

"I don't know exactly. I'm not quite sure. Yes, I think I thought perhaps you'd come. But oh! if you please, Monsieur Dudu," he exclaimed, suddenly starting up, "do let me go and call Jeanne. I promised her I would if you came, or if I saw anything funny. Do let me go. I won't be a minute."

But the raven cocked his head on one side and looked at Hugh rather sternly.

"No," he said. "You cannot go for Jeanne. I do not wish it at present."

Hugh felt rather angry. Why should Dudu lay down the law to him in this way?

"But I promised," he began.

"People should not promise what they are not sure of being able to perform," he said sententiously. "Besides, even if you did go to get Jeanne, she couldn't come. She is ever so far away."

"Away!" repeated Hugh in amazement, "away! Little Jeanne gone away. Oh no, you must be joking Du—, I beg your pardon, Monsieur Dudu."

"Not at all," said Dudu. "She *is* away, and farther away than you or she has any notion of, even though if you went into her room you would see her little rosy face lying on the pillow. *She* is away."

Hugh still looked puzzled, though rather less so.

"You mean that her thinking is away, I suppose," he said. "But I could wake her."

Again the raven cocked his head on one side.

"No," he said. "You must be content to do my way at present. Now, tell me what it is you want. Why did you wish me to come to see you?"

"I wanted—at least I thought, and Jeanne said so," began Hugh. "We thought perhaps you were a fairy, Monsieur Dudu, and that you could take us into the castle in the tapestry. It looked so bright and real a few minutes ago," he added, turning to the wall, which was now only faintly illumined by the moonlight, and looked no different from what Hugh had often seen it in the daytime. "What has become of the beautiful light, Monsieur Dudu? And the peacocks? They have shut up their tails again——"

"Never mind," said the raven. "So you want to see the castle, do you?" he added.

"Yes," said Hugh; "but not so much as Jeanne. It was she wanted it most. She wants dreadfully to see it. *I* thought," he added, rather timidly, "*I* thought we might play at giving a party in the castle, and inviting Houpet, you know, and Nibble."

"*Only*," observed the raven, drily, "there is one little objection to that. *Generally*—I may be mistaken, of course, my notions are very old-fashioned, I daresay—but, *generally*, people give parties in their own houses, don't they?"

And as he spoke he looked straight at Hugh, cocking his head on one side more than ever.

CHAPTER IV.

THE FOREST OF THE RAINBOWS.

"Rose and amethyst, gold and grey."
"ONCE."

HUGH felt rather offended. It was natural that he should do so, I think. At least I am sure that in his place I too should have felt hurt. He had said nothing to make the raven speak in that disagreeably sarcastic way.

"I wish Jeanne were here," he said to himself; "she would think of something to put him down a little."

But aloud he said nothing, so, great was his surprise, when the raven coolly remarked in answer to his unspoken thoughts,

"So Jeanne could put me down, you think? I confess, I don't agree with you. However, never mind about that. We shall be very good friends in time. And now, how about visiting the castle?"

"I should like to go," replied Hugh, thinking it wiser, all things considered, to get over his offended feelings. "I should like to see the castle very much, though I should have liked Jeanne to be with me; but still," he went on, reflecting that Jeanne would be extremely disappointed if he did not make the most of his present opportunity, such as it was, "if you will be so kind as to show me the way, Monsieur Dudu, I'd like to go, and then, any way, I can tell Jeanne all about it."

"I cannot exactly show you the way," said the raven, "I am only the guardian on this side. But if you will attend to what I say, you will get on very well. Here, in the first place, is a pair of wall-climbers to put on your feet."

He held out his claw, on the end of which hung, by a narrow ribbon, two round little cushions about the size of a macaroon biscuit. Hugh took them, and examined them curiously. They were soft and elastic, what Hugh in his own words would have described as "blobby." They seemed to be made of some stuff like indiarubber, and were just the colour of his skin.

"What funny things!" said Hugh.

"They are made after the pattern of the fly's wall-climbers," remarked the raven. "Put them on—tie them on, that is to say, so that they will be just in the middle of your foot, underneath of course. That's right; now jump out of bed and follow me," and before Hugh knew what he was doing he found himself walking with the greatest ease straight up the wall to where the long flight of steps to the tapestry castle began. On the lowest steps the raven stopped a moment.

"Shall I take them off now?" asked Hugh. "I don't need them to walk up steps with."

"Take them off?" said the raven; "oh dear no. When you don't need them they won't incommode you, and they'll be all ready for the next time. Besides, though it mayn't seem so to you, these steps are not so easy to get up as you think. At least they wouldn't be without the wall-climbers."

With them, however, nothing could have been easier. Hugh found himself in no time at the top of the flight of steps in front of the door from which the raven had come out. The peacocks, now he was close to them, seemed to him larger than ordinary peacocks, but the brilliant colours of their feathers, which he had noticed in the bright moonlight, had disappeared. It was light enough for him to distinguish their figures, but that was all.

"I must leave you now," said the raven; "but

you will get on very well. Only remember these two things—don't be impatient, and don't take off your wall-climbers; and if you are very much at a loss about anything, call me."

"How shall I call you?" asked Hugh.

"Whistle softly three times. Now, I think it is time to light up. Peacocks."

The peacocks, one on each side of the door, came forward solemnly, saluting the raven with the greatest respect.

"Ring," said the raven, and to Hugh's surprise each peacock lifted up a claw, and taking hold of a bell-rope, of which there were two, one on each side of the door, pulled them vigorously. No sound ensued, but at the instant there burst forth the same soft yet brilliant light which had so delighted Hugh when he first awoke, and which he now discovered to come not from the moon, still shining in gently at the window of the tapestry room down below, but from those of the castle at whose door he was standing. He had never before noticed how many windows it had. Jeanne and he had only remarked the door at the top of the steps, but now the light which flowed out from above him was so clear and brilliant that it seemed as if the whole castle must be transparent. Hugh stood in eager expectation of what was to happen next, and was on the point of speaking to the raven, standing, as he thought, beside him, when a sudden sound made him turn round. It was that of the castle door opening, and at the same moment the two peacocks, coming forward, pushed him gently, one at each side, so that Hugh found himself obliged to enter. He was by no means unwilling to do so, but he gave one last look round for his conductor. He was gone.

For about half a second Hugh felt a little frightened and bewildered.

"I wish Dudu had come with me," he said. But almost before he had time to think the wish, what he saw before him so absorbed his attention that he forgot everything else.

It was a long, long passage, high in the roof, though narrow of course in comparison with its length, but wide enough for Hugh—for Hugh and Jeanne hand-in-hand even—to walk along with perfect comfort and great satisfaction, for oh, it was so prettily lighted up! You have, I daresay, children, often admired in London or Paris, or some great town, the rows of gas lamps lighting up at night miles of some very long street. Fancy those lights infinitely brighter and clearer, and yet softer than any lamps you ever saw, and each one of a different colour, from the richest crimson to the softest pale blue, and you will have some idea how pretty the long corridor before him looked to Hugh. He stepped along delightedly, as well he might. "Why, this of itself is worth staying awake ever so many nights to see," he said to himself; "only I do wish Jeanne were with me."

Where did the corridor lead to? He ran on and on for some time without thinking much about this, so interested was he in observing the lamps and the pretty way in which the tints were arranged; but after a while he began to find it a little monotonous, especially when he noticed that at long intervals the colours repeated themselves, the succession of shades beginning again from time to time.

"I shall learn them by heart if I go on here much longer," thought Hugh. "I think I'll sit down a little to rest. Not that I feel tired of walking, but I may as well sit down a little."

He did so—on the ground, there was nothing else to sit on—and then a very queer thing happened. The lamps took to moving instead of him, so that when he looked up at them the impression was just the same as when he himself had been running along. The colours succeeded each other in the same order, and Hugh began to wonder whether his eyes were not deceiving him in some queer way.

"Anyhow, I'll run on a little farther," he said to himself, "and if I don't come to the end of this passage soon, I'll run back again to the other end. It feels just as if I had got inside a kaleidoscope."

He hastened on, and was beginning really to think of turning back again and running the other way, when, all of a sudden—everything in this queer tapestry world he had got into seemed to happen all of a sudden—a little bell was heard to ring, clear and silvery, but not very loud, and in another instant—oh dear!—all the pretty coloured lamps were extinguished, and poor Hugh was left standing all in the dark. Where he was he did not know, what to do he did not know; had he not been eight years old on his last birthday I almost think he would have begun to cry. He felt, too, all of a sudden so cold, even though before he had got out of bed he had taken the precaution to put on his red flannel dressing-gown, and till now had felt quite pleasantly warm. It was only for half a moment, however, that the idea of crying came over him.

"I'm very glad poor little Jeanne isn't here," he said to himself by way of keeping up his own courage; "she *would* have been afraid. But as I'm a boy it doesn't matter. I'll just try to find my way all the same. I suppose it's some trick of that Dudu's."

He felt his way along bravely for a few minutes, and more bravely still was forcing back his tears, when a sound caught his ears. It was a cock's crow, sharp and shrill, but yet sounding as if outside the place where he was. Still it greatly encouraged Hugh, who continued to make his way on in the dark, much pleased to find that the farther he got the nearer and clearer sounded the crow, repeated every few seconds. And at last he found himself at the end of the passage—he knew it must be so, for in front of him the way was barred, and *quite* close to him now apparently, sounded the cock's shrill call. He pushed and pulled—for some time in vain. If there were a door at this end of the passage, as surely there must be—who would make a passage and hang it so beautifully with lamps if it were to lead to nowhere?—it was a door of which the handle was very difficult to find.

"Oh dear!" exclaimed Hugh, half in despair, "what shall I do?"

"Kurroo—kurroorulloo," sounded the cock's crow. "Try again," it seemed to say, encouragingly. And at last Hugh's hand came in contact with a little round knob, and as he touched it, all at once everything about him was lighted up again with the same clear, lovely light coming from the thousands of lamps down the long corridor behind him. But Hugh never turned to look at them—what he saw in front of him was so delightful and surprising.

The door had opened, Hugh found himself standing at the top of two or three steps, which apparently were the back approach to the strange long passage which he had entered from the tapestry room. Outside it was light too, but not with the wonderful bright radiance that had streamed out from the castle at the other side. Here it was just very soft, very clear moonlight. There were trees before him—almost it seemed as if he were standing at the entrance of a forest. But, strange to say, they were not winter trees, such as he had left behind him in the garden of Jeanne's house—bare and leafless, or if covered at all, covered only with their Christmas dress of snow and icicles—these trees were clothed with the loveliest foliage, fresh and green and feathery, which no winter's storms or nipping frosts had ever come near to blight. And in the little space between the door where Hugh stood and these wonderful trees was drawn up, as if awaiting him, the prettiest, queerest, most delicious little carriage that ever was seen. It was open; the cushions with which it was lined were of rose-coloured plush—not velvet, I think; at least if they *were* velvet, it was of some marvellous kind that couldn't be rubbed the wrong way, that felt exquisitely smooth and soft whichever way you stroked it; the body of the carriage was shaped something like a cockle-shell; you could lie back in it so beautifully without cricking or straining your neck or shoulders in the least; and there was just room for two. One of these two was already comfortably settled—shall I tell you who it was now, or shall I keep it for a tit-bit at the end when I have quite finished about the carriage? Yes, that will be better. For the funniest things about the carriage have to be told yet. Up on the box, in the coachman's place, you understand, holding with an air of the utmost importance in one claw a pair of yellow silk reins, his tufted head surmounted by a gold-laced livery hat, which, however, must have had a hole in the middle to let the tuft through, for there it was in all its glory waving over the hat like a dragoon's plume, sat, or stood rather, Houpet; while, standing behind, holding on each with one claw to the back of the carriage, like real footmen, were the two other chickens. They, too, had gold-laced hats and an air of solemn propriety, not *quite* so majestic as Houpet's, for in their case the imposing tuft was wanting, but still very fine of its kind. And who do you think were the horses? for there were two—or, to speak more correctly, there were no horses at all, but in the place where they should have been were harnessed, tandem-fashion, not abreast, Nibble the guinea-pig and Grignan the tortoise! Nibble next the carriage, Grignan, of all creatures in the world, as leader.

On sight of them Hugh began to laugh, so that he forgot to look more closely at the person in the carriage, whose face he had not yet seen, as it was turned the other way. But the sound of his laughing was too infectious to be resisted—the small figure began to shake all over, and at last could contain itself no longer. With a shout of merriment little Jeanne, for it was she, sprang out of the carriage and threw her arms round Hugh's neck.

"O Chéri," she said, "I *couldn't* keep quiet any longer, though I wanted to hide my face till you had got into the carriage, and then surprise you. But it was so nice to hear you laugh — I *couldn't* keep still."

Hugh felt too utterly astonished to reply. He just stared at Jeanne as if he could not believe his own eyes. And Jeanne did not look surprised at all! That, to Hugh, was the most surprising part of the whole.

"Jeanne!" he exclaimed, "you here! Why, Dudu told me you were ever so far away."

"And so I am," replied Jeanne, laughing again, "and so are you, Chéri. You have no idea how far away you are—miles, and miles, and miles, only in this country they don't have milestones. It's all quite different."

"How do you mean?" asked Hugh. "How do you know all about it? You have never been here before, have you? I couldn't quite understand Dudu—*he* meant, I think, that it was only your thinking part or your fancying part, that was away."

Jeanne laughed again. Hugh felt a little impatient.

"*Jeanne*," he said, "do leave off laughing and speak to me. What is this place? and how did you come here? and have you ever been here before?"

"Yes," said Jeanne, "I think so; but I don't know

how I came. And I don't want to do anything but laugh and have fun. Never mind how we came. It's a beautiful country, any way, and did you *ever* see anything so sweet as the little carriage they've sent for us, and wasn't it nice to see Houpet and all the others?"

"Yes," said Hugh, "very. But whom do you mean by 'they,' Jeanne?"

"Oh dear, dear!" exclaimed Jeanne, "what a terrible boy you are. Do leave off asking questions, and let us have fun. Look, there are Grignan and the little cochon quite eager to be off. Now, do jump in—we shall have such fun."

Hugh got in, willingly enough, though still he would have preferred to have some explanation from Jeanne of all the strange things that were happening.

"*Isn't* it nice?" said Jeanne, when they had both nestled down among the delicious soft cushions of the carriage.

"Yes," said Hugh, "it's very nice *now*, but it wasn't very nice when I was all alone in the dark in that long passage. As you seem to know all about everything, Jeanne, I suppose you know about that."

He spoke rather, just a very little, grumpily, but Jeanne, rather to his surprise, did not laugh at him this time. Instead, she looked up in his face earnestly, with a strange deep look in her eyes.

"I think very often we have to find our way in the dark," she said dreamily. "I think I remember about that. But," she went on, with a complete change of voice, her eyes dancing merrily as if they had never looked grave in their life, "it's not dark now, Chéri, and it's going to be ever so bright. Just look at the lovely moon through the trees. Do let us go now. Gee-up, gee-up, crack your whip, Houpet, and make them gallop as fast as you can."

Off they set—they went nice and fast certainly, but not so fast but that the children could admire the beautiful feathery foliage as they passed. They drove through the forest—for the trees that Hugh had so admired were those of a forest—on and on, swiftly but yet smoothly; never in his life had Hugh felt any motion so delightful.

"*What* a good coachman Houpet is!" exclaimed Hugh. "I never should have thought he could drive so well. How does he know the road, Jeanne?"

"There isn't any road, so he doesn't need to know it," said Jeanne. "Look before you, Chéri. You see there is no road. It makes itself as we go, so we can't go wrong."

Hugh looked straight before him. It was as Jeanne had said. The trees grew thick and close in front, only dividing—melting away like a mist—as the quaint little carriage approached them.

Hugh looked at them with fresh surprise.

"Are they not real trees?" he said.

"Of course they are," said Jeanne. "Now they're beginning to change; that shows we are getting to the middle of the forest. Look, look, Chéri!"

Hugh "looked" with all his eyes. What Jeanne called "changing" was a very wonderful process. The trees, which hitherto had been of a very bright, delicate green, began gradually to pale in colour, becoming first greenish-yellow, then canary colour, then down to the purest white. And from white they grew into silver, sparkling like innumerable diamonds, and then slowly altered into a sort of silver-grey, gradually rising into grey-blue, then into a more purple-blue, till they reached the richest corn-flower shade. Then began another series of lessening shades, which again, passing through a boundary line of gold, rose by indescribable degrees to deep yet brilliant crimson. It would be impossible to name all the variations through which they passed. I use the names of the colours and shades which are familiar to you, children, but the very naming any shade gives an unfair idea of the marvellous delicacy with which one tint melted into another,—as well try to divide and mark off the hues of a dove's breast, or of the sky at sunset. And all the time the trees themselves were of the same form and foliage as at first, the leaves—or fronds I feel inclined to call them, for they were more like very, very delicate ferns or ferny grass than leaves — with which each branch was luxuriantly clothed, seeming to bathe themselves in each new colour as the petals of a flower welcome a flood of brilliant sunshine.

"Oh, how pretty!" said Hugh, with a deep sigh of pleasure. "It is like the lamps, only much prettier. I think, Jeanne, this must be the country of pretty colours."

"This forest is called the Forest of the Rainbows. I know *that*," said Jeanne. "But I don't think they call this the country of pretty colours, Chéri. You see it is the country of so many pretty things. If we lived in it always, we should never see the end of the beautiful things there are. Only——"

"Only what?" asked Hugh.

"I don't think it would be a good plan to live in it always. Just sometimes is best, I think. Either the things wouldn't be so pretty, or our eyes wouldn't see them so well after a while. But see, Chéri, the trees are growing common-coloured again, and Houpet is stopping. We must have got to the end of the Forest of the Rainbows."

"And where shall we be going to now?" asked Hugh. "Must we get out, do you think, Jeanne? Oh, listen, I hear the sound of water! Do you hear it, Jeanne? There must be a river near here. I wish the moonlight was a little brighter. Now that the trees don't shine, it seems quite dull. But oh, how plainly I hear the water. Listen, Jeanne, don't you hear it too?"

"Yes," said Jeanne. "It must be——" but before she had time to say more they suddenly came out of the enchanted forest; in an instant every trace of the feathery trees had disappeared. Houpet pulled up his steeds, the two chickens got down from behind, and stood one on each side of the carriage door, waiting apparently for their master and mistress to descend. And plainer and nearer than before came the sound of fast-rushing water.

"You see we are to get down," said Hugh.

"Yes," said Jeanne again, looking round her a little timidly. "Chéri, do you know, I feel just a very,

very little bit frightened. It is such a queer place, and I don't know what we should do. Don't you think we'd better ask Houpet to take us back again?"

"Oh no," said Hugh. "I'm sure we'll be all right. You said you wanted to have some fun, Jeanne, and you seemed to know all about it. You needn't be frightened with *me*, Jeanne."

"No, of course not," said Jeanne, quite brightly again; "but let us stand up a minute, Hugh, before we get out of the carriage, and look all about us. *Isn't* it a queer place?"

"It" was a wide, far-stretching plain, over which the moonlight shone softly. Far or near not a shrub or tree was to be seen, yet it was not like a desert, for the ground was entirely covered with most beautiful moss, so fresh and green, even by the moonlight, that it was difficult to believe the hot sunshine had ever glared upon it. And here and there, all over this great plain—all over it, at least, as far as the children could see—rose suddenly from the ground innumerable jets of water, not so much like fountains as like little waterfalls turned the wrong way; they rushed upwards with such surprising force and noise, and fell to the earth again in numberless tiny threads much more gently and softly than they left it.

"It seems as if somebody must be shooting them up with a gun, doesn't it?" said Hugh. "I never saw such queer fountains."

"Let's go and look at them close," said Jeanne, preparing to get down. But before she could do so, Houpet gave a shrill, rather peremptory crow, and Jeanne stopped short in surprise.

"What do you want, Houpet?" she said.

By way of reply, Houpet hopped down from his box, and in some wonderfully clever way of his own, before the children could see what he was about, had unharnessed Nibble and Grignan. Then the three arranged themselves in a little procession, and drew up a few steps from the side of the carriage where still stood the chicken-footmen. Though they could not speak, there was no mistaking their meaning.

"They're going to show us the way," said Hugh; and as he spoke he jumped out of the carriage, and Jeanne after him.

ONWARDS QUIETLY STEPPED THE LITTLE PROCESSION.—p. 75.

CHAPTER V.

FROG-LAND.

"They have a pretty island,
Whereon at night they rest;
They have a sparkling lakelet,
And float upon its breast."

THE TWO SWANS.

ONWARDS quietly stepped the little procession, Houpet first, his tuft waving as usual, with a comfortable air of importance and satisfaction; then Nibble and Grignan abreast—hand-in-hand, I was going to have said; next Hugh and Jeanne; with the two attendant chickens behind bringing up the rear.

"I wonder where they are going to take us to," said Hugh in a low voice. Somehow the soft light; the strange loneliness of the great plain, where, now that they were accustomed to it, the rushing of the numberless water-springs seemed to be but one single, steady sound; the solemn behaviour of their curious guides, altogether, had subdued the children's spirits. Jeanne said no more about "having fun," yet she did not seem the least frightened or depressed; she was only quiet and serious.

"Where *do* you think they are going to take us to?" repeated Hugh.

"I don't know—at least I'm not sure," said Jeanne; "but, Chéri, isn't it a good thing that Houpet and the others are with us to show us the way, for though the ground looks so pretty it is quite boggy here and there. I notice that Houpet never goes quite close to the fountains, and just when I went the least bit near one a minute ago my feet began to slip down."

"I haven't felt it like that at all," said Hugh. "Perhaps it's because of my wall-climbers. Dudu gave me a pair of wall-climbers like the flies', you know, Jeanne."

"Did he?" said Jeanne, not at all surprised, and as if wall-climbers were no more uncommon than goloshes. "He didn't give me any, but then I came a different way from you. I think every one comes a different way to this country, do you know, Chéri?"

"And very likely Dudu thought I could carry you if there was anywhere you couldn't climb," said Hugh, importantly. "I'm sure I——" he stopped abruptly, for a sudden crow from Houpet had brought all the party to a standstill. At first the children could not make out why their guide had stopped here—there was nothing to be seen. But pressing forward a few steps to where Houpet stood, Hugh saw, imbedded in the moss at his feet, a stone with a ring in it, just like those which one reads of in the *Arabian Nights.* Houpet stood at the edge of the stone eyeing it gravely, and somehow he managed to make Hugh understand that he was to lift it. Nothing loth, but rather doubtful as to whether he would be strong enough, the boy leant forward to reach the ring, first whispering, however, to Jeanne,

"It's getting like a quite real fairy tale, isn't it, Jeanne?"

Jeanne nodded, but looked rather anxious.

"I'm *afraid* you can't lift it, Chéri," she said. "I think I'd better stand behind and pull *you*—the ring isn't big enough for us both to put our hands in it."

Hugh made no objection to her proposal, so Jeanne put her arms round his waist, and when he gave a great pug to the ring she gave a great pug to him. The first time it was no use, the stone did not move in the least.

"Try again," said Hugh, and try again they did. But no—the second try succeeded no better than the first—and the children looked at each other in perplexity. Suddenly there was a movement among the animals, who had all been standing round watching the children's attempts; Jeanne felt a sort of little pecking tug at her skirts—how it came about I cannot say, but I think I forgot to tell you that, unlike Hugh in his red flannel dressing gown, *she* was arrayed for their adventures in her best Sunday pelisse, trimmed with fur—and, looking round, lo and behold! there was Houpet holding on to her with his beak, then came Nibble, his two front paws embracing Houpet's feathered body, Grignan behind him again, clutching with his mouth at Nibble's fur, and the two chickens at the end holding on to Grignan and each other in some indescribable and marvellous way. It was, for all the world, as if they were preparing for the finish-up part of the game of "oranges and lemons," or for that of "fox and geese!"

The sight was so comical that it was all the children could do to keep their gravity, they succeeded in doing so, however, fearing that it might hurt the animals' feelings to seem to make fun of their well-meant efforts.

"Not that *they* can be any use," whispered Hugh "but it's very good-natured of them all the same."

"I am not so sure that they can't be of any use," returned Jeanne. "Think of how well Houpet drove."

"Here goes, then," said Hugh. "One, two, *three;*" and with "three" he gave a tremendous tug—a much more tremendous tug than was required, for, to his surprise, the stone yielded at once without the slightest resistance, and back they all fell, one on the top of the other, Hugh, Jeanne, Houpet, Nibble, Grignan, and the two chickens! But none of them were any the worse, and with the greatest eagerness to see what was to be seen where the stone had been, up jumped Hugh and Jeanne and ran forward to the spot.

"There should be," said Jeanne, half out of breath—"there *should* be a little staircase for us to go down, if it is like the stories in the *Arabian Nights.*"

And, wonderful to relate, so there was! The children could hardly believe their eyes, when below them they saw the most tempting little spiral staircase of white stone or marble steps, with a neat little brass balustrade at one side. It looked quite light all the way down, though of course they could distinguish nothing at the bottom, as the corkscrew twists of the staircase entirely filled up the space.

Houpet hopped forward and stood at the top of the steps crowing softly.

"He means that we're to go down," said Hugh. "Shall we?"

"Of course," said Jeanne. "I'm not a bit afraid. We won't have any fun if we don't go on."

"Well then," said Hugh, "I'll go first as I'm a boy, just *in case,* you know, Jeanne, of our meeting anything disagreeable."

So down he went, Jeanne following close after.

"I suppose Houpet and the others will come after us," said Jeanne, rather anxiously. But just as she uttered the words a rather shrill crow made both Hugh and her stop short and look up to the top. They saw Houpet and the others standing round the edge of the hole. Houpet gave another crow, in which the two chickens joined him, and then suddenly the stone was shut down—the two children found themselves alone in this strange place, leading to they knew not where! Jeanne gave a little cry—Hugh, too, for a moment was rather startled, but he soon recovered himself.

"Jeanne," he said, "it must be all right. I don't think we need be frightened. See, it is quite light! The light comes up from below—down there it must be quite bright and cheerful. Give me your hand—if we go down sideways—so—we can hold each other's hands all the way."

So, in a rather queer fashion, they clambered down the long staircase. By the time they got to its end they were really quite tired of turning round and round so many times. But now the view before them was so pleasant that they forgot all their troubles.

They had found a little door at the foot of the stair, which opened easily. They passed through it, and there lay before them a beautiful expanse of water surrounded by hills; the door which had closed behind them seemed on this side to have been cut out of the turf of the hill, and was all but invisible. It was light, as Hugh had said, but not with the light of either sun or moon; a soft radiance was over everything, but whence it came they could not tell. The hills on each side of the water, which was more like a calmly flowing river than a lake, prevented their seeing very far, but close to the shore by which they stood a little boat was moored—a little boat with seats for two, and one light pair of oars.

"Oh, how lovely!" said Jeanne. "It is even nicer than the carriage. Get in, Hugh, and let us row down the river. The boat must be on purpose for us."

They were soon settled in it, and Hugh, though he had only rowed once or twice before in his life, found it very easy and pleasant, and they went over the water swiftly and smoothly. After a while the hills approached more nearly, gradually the broad river dwindled to a mere stream, so narrow and small at last, that even their tiny boat could go no farther. Hugh was forced to leave off rowing.

"I suppose we are meant to go on shore here," he said. "The boat won't go any farther, any way."

Jeanne was peering forward: just before them the brook, or what still remained of it, almost disappeared in a narrow little gorge between the hills.

"Chéri," said she, "I shouldn't wonder if the stream gets wider again on the other side of this little narrow place. Don't you think we'd better try to pull the boat through, and then we might get into it again?"

"Perhaps," said Hugh. "We may try." So out the children got—Jeanne pulled in front, Hugh pushed behind. It was so very light that there was no difficulty as to its weight; only the gorge was so narrow that at last the boat stuck fast.

"We'd better leave it and clamber through ourselves," said Hugh.

"But, O Chéri, we can't!" cried Jeanne. "From where I am I can see that the water gets wider again a little farther on. And the rocks come quite sharp down to the side. There is nowhere we could clamber on to, and I dare say the water is very deep. There are lots of little streams trickling into it from the rocks, and the boat could go quite well if we could but get it a little farther."

"But we can't," said Hugh; "it just won't go."

"Oh dear," said Jeanne, "we'll have to go back. But how should we find the door in the hillside to go up the stair; or if we did get up, how should we push away the stone? And even then, there would be the forest to go through, and perhaps we couldn't find our way among the trees as Houpet did. O Chéri, what shall we do?"

Hugh stood still and considered.

"I think," he said at last, "I think the time's come for whistling."

And before Jeanne could ask him what he meant, he gave three clear, short whistles, and then waited to see the effect.

It was a most unexpected one. Hugh had anticipated nothing else than the sudden appearance, somehow and somewhere, of Monsieur Dudu himself, as large as life—possibly, in this queer country of surprises, where they found themselves, a little larger! When and how he would appear Hugh was perfectly at a loss to imagine—he might fly down from the sky;

he might spring up from the water; he might just suddenly stand before them without their having any idea how he had come. Hugh laughed to himself at the thought of Jeanne's astonishment, and after all it was Jeanne who first drew his attention to what was really happening.

"Hark, Chéri, hark!" she cried, "what a queer noise! What can it be?"

Hugh's attention had been so taken up in staring about in every direction for the raven that he had not noticed the sound which Jeanne had heard, and which now increased every moment.

It was a soft, swishy sound—as if innumerable little boats were making their way through water, or as if innumerable little fairies were bathing themselves, only every instant it came nearer and nearer, till at last, on every side of the boat in which the children were still standing, came creeping up from below lots and lots and *lots* of small, bright green frogs, who clambered over the sides and arranged themselves in lines along the edges in the most methodical and orderly manner. Jeanne gave a scream of horror, and darted across the boat to where Hugh was standing.

"O Chéri," she cried, "why did you whistle?

It's all that naughty Dudu. He's going to turn us into frogs too, I do believe, because he thinks I laughed at him. Oh dear, oh dear, what shall we do?"

Chéri himself, though not quite so frightened as Jeanne, was not much pleased with the result of his summons to the raven.

"It does look like a shabby trick," he said; "but still I do not think the creatures mean to do us any harm. And I don't feel myself being turned into a frog yet; do you, Jeanne?"

"I don't know," said Jeanne, a very little comforted; "I don't know what it would feel like to be turned into a frog; I've always been a little girl, and so I can't tell. I feel rather creepy and chilly, but perhaps it's only with seeing the frogs. What funny red eyes they've got. What can they be going to do?"

She forgot her fears in the interest of watching them; Hugh, too, stared with all his eyes at the frogs, who, arranged in regular lines round the edge of the boat, began working away industriously at something which, for a minute or two, the children could not make out. At last Jeanne called out eagerly,

"They are throwing over little lines, Chéri—lots

and lots of little lines. There must be frogs down below waiting to catch them."

So it was; each frog threw over several threads which he seemed to unwind from his body; these threads were caught by something invisible down below, and twisted round and round several times, till at last they became as firm and strong as a fine twine. And when, apparently, the frogs considered that they had made cables enough, they settled themselves down, each firmly on his two hind legs, still holding by the rope with their front ones, and then—in another moment—to the children's great delight, they felt the boat beginning to move. It moved on smoothly—almost as smoothly as when on the water—there were no jogs or tugs, as might have been the case if it had been pulled by two or three coarse, strong ropes, for all the hundreds of tiny cables pulling together made one even force.

"Why, how clever they are!" cried Jeanne. "We go as smoothly as if we were on wheels. Nice little frogs. I am sure we are very much obliged to them—aren't we, Chéri?"

"And to Dudu," observed Hugh.

Jeanne shrugged her shoulders. She was not over and above sure of Dudu even now.

The boat moved along for some time; the pass between the hills was dark and gloomy, and though the water got wider, as Jeanne had seen, it would not for some distance have been possible for the children to row After a time it suddenly grew much lighter; they came out from the narrow pass and found themselves but a few yards from a sheet of still water, with trees all round it—a sort of mountain lake it seemed, silent and solitary, and reflecting back from its calm bosom the soft, silvery, even radiance which since they came out from the door on the hillside had been the children's only light.

And in the middle of this lake lay a little island —a perfect nest of trees, whose long drooping branches hung down into the water.

"Oh, do let us row on to the island," said Jeanne eagerly, for by this time the frogs had drawn them to the edge of the lake; there could no longer be any difficulty in rowing for themselves.

"First, any way, we must thank the frogs," said Hugh, standing up. He would have taken off his cap if he had had one on; as it was, he could only bow politely.

As he did so, each frog turned round so as to face him, and each gave a little bob of the head, which.

though not very graceful, was evidently meant as an acknowledgment of Hugh's courtesy.

"They are very polite frogs," whispered Hugh. "Jeanne, do stand up and bow to them too."

Jeanne, who all this time had been sitting with her feet tucked up under her, showed no inclination to move.

"I don't like to stand up," she said, "for fear the frogs should run up my legs. But I can thank them just as well sitting down. Frogs," she added, "frogs, I am very much obliged to you, and I hope you will excuse my not standing up."

The frogs bowed again, which was very considerate of them; then suddenly there seemed a movement among them, those at the end of the boat drew back a little, and a frog, whom the children had not hitherto specially observed, came forward and stood in front of the others. He was bigger, his colour was a brighter green, and his eyes more brilliantly red. He stood up on his hind legs and bowed politely. Then, after clearing his throat, of which there was much need, for even with this precaution it sounded very croaky, he addressed the children.

"Monsieur and Mademoiselle," he began, "are very welcome to what we have done for them—the small service we have rendered. Monsieur and Mademoiselle, I and my companions"—"He should say, 'My companions and I,'" whispered Jeanne—"are well brought up frogs. We know our place in society. We disapprove of newfangled notions. We are frogs—we desire to be nothing else, and we are deeply sensible of the honour Monsieur and Mademoiselle have done us by this visit."

"He really speaks very nicely," said Jeanne in a whisper.

"Before Monsieur and Mademoiselle bid us farewell—before they leave our shores," continued the frog with a wave of his "top legs," as Jeanne afterwards called them, "we should desire to give them what, without presumption, I may call a treat. Monsieur and Mademoiselle are, doubtless, aware that in our humble way we are artists. Our weakness—our strength I should rather say—is music. Our croaking concerts are renowned far and wide, and by a most fortunate coincidence one is about to take place, to celebrate the farewell—the departure to other regions—of a songster whose family fame for many ages has been renowned. Monsieur and Mademoiselle, to-night is to be heard for the first time in this century the 'Song of the Swan.'"

"The song of the swan," repeated Hugh, rather puzzled; "I didn't know swans ever sang. I thought it was just an old saying that they sing once only—when they are dying."

The frog bowed.

"Just so," he said; "it is the truth. And, therefore, the extreme difficulty of assisting at so unique a performance. It is but seldom—not above half-a-dozen times in the recollection of the oldest of my venerated cousins, the toads, that such an opportunity has occurred—and as to whether human ears have *ever* before been regaled with what you are about to enjoy, you must allow me, Monsieur and Mademoiselle, with all deference to your race, for whom naturally we cherish the highest respect, to express a doubt."

"It's a little difficult to understand quite what he means, isn't it, Chéri?" whispered Jeanne. "But, of course, we mustn't say so. It might hurt his feelings."

"Yes," agreed Hugh, "it might. But we must say something polite."

"You say it," said Jeanne. "I really daren't stand up, and it's not so easy to make a speech sitting down."

"Monsieur Frog, we are very much obliged to you," began Hugh. "Please tell all the other frogs so too.

We would like very much to hear the concert. When does it begin, and where will it be?"

"All round the lake the performers will be stationed," replied the frog pompously. "The chief artist occupies the island which you see from here. If you move forward a little—to about half-way between the shore and the island—you will, I think, be excellently placed. But first," seeing that Hugh was preparing to take up the oars, "first, you will allow us, Monsieur and Mademoiselle, to offer you a little collation—some slight refreshment after all the fatigues of your journey to our shores."

"Oh dear! oh dear!" whispered Jeanne in a terrible fright; "please say 'No, thank you,' Chéri. I *know* they'll be bringing us that horrid green stuff for soup."

"Thank you very much," said Hugh; "you are very kind indeed, Monsieur Frog, only, really, we're not hungry."

"A little refreshment—a mere nothing," said the frog, waving his hands in an elegantly persuasive manner. "Tadpoles"—in a brisk, authoritative tone—"tadpoles, refreshments for our guests."

Jeanne shivered, but nevertheless could not help watching with curiosity. Scores of little tadpoles came hopping up the sides of the boat, each dozen or so of them carrying among them large water-lily leaves, on each of which curious and dainty-looking little cakes and bonbons were arranged. The first that was presented to Jeanne contained neat little biscuits about the size of a half-crown piece, of a tempting rich brown colour.

"Flag-flour cakes," said the frog. "We roast and grind the flour in our own mills. You will find them good."

Jeanne took one and found it very good. She would have taken another, but already a second tray-ful or leaf-ful was before her, with pinky-looking balls.

"Those are made from the sugar of water-brambles," remarked the frog, with a self-satisfied smile. "No doubt you are surprised at the delicacy and refinement of our tastes. Many human beings are under the deplorable mistake of supposing we live on slimy water and dirty insects—ha, ha, ha! whereas our cuisine is astounding in variety and delicacy of material and flavour. If it were not too late in the season, I wish you could have tasted our mushroom pâtés and minnows' eggs vols-au-vent."

"Thank you," said Hugh, "what we have had is very nice indeed."

"I *couldn't* eat minnows' eggs," whispered Jeanne, looking rather doubtfully at the succession of leaf trays that continued to appear. She nibbled away at some of the least extraordinary-looking cakes, which the frog informed her were made from the pith of rushes roasted and ground down, and then flavoured with essence of marsh marigold, and found them nearly as nice as macaroons. Then, having eaten quite as much as they wanted, the tadpoles handed to each a leaf of the purest water, which they drank with great satisfaction.

"Now," said Hugh, "we're quite ready for the concert. Shall I row out to the middle of the lake, Monsieur Frog?"

"Midway between the shore and the island," said the frog; "that will be the best position;" and, as by this time all the frogs that had been sitting round the edge of the boat had disappeared, Hugh took the oars and paddled away.

CHAPTER VI.

THE SONG OF THE SWAN.

"—— If I were on that shore,
I should live there and not die, but sing evermore.'
JEAN INGELOW.

"ABOUT here will do, I should think—eh, Monsieur Frog?" said Hugh, resting on his oars half-way to the island. But there was no answer. The frog had disappeared.

"What a queer way all these creatures behave, don't they, Jeanne?" he said. "First Dudu, then Houpet and the others. They go off all of a sudden in the oddest way."

"I suppose they have to go when we don't need them any more," said Jeanne. "I daresay they are obliged to."

"Who obliges them?" said Hugh.

"Oh, I don't know! The fairies, I suppose," said Jeanne.

"Was it the fairies you meant when you kept saying 'they'?" asked Hugh.

"I don't know—perhaps—it's no use asking me," said Jeanne. "Fairies, or dream-spirits, or something like that. Never mind who they are if they give us nice things. I am sure the frogs have been *very* kind, haven't they?"

"Yes; you won't be so afraid of them now, will you, Jeanne?"

"Oh, I don't know. I daresay I shall be, for they're quite different from *our* frogs. Ours aren't so bright green, and their eyes aren't red, and they can't *talk*. Oh no, our frogs are quite different from *theirs*, Chéri," she added with profound conviction.

"Just like our trees and everything else, I suppose," said Hugh. "Certainly this is a funny country. But hush, Jeanne! I believe the concert's going to begin."

They sat perfectly still to listen, but for a minute or two the sound which had caught Hugh's attention was not repeated. Everything about them was silent, except that now and then a soft faint breeze seemed to flutter across the water, slightly rippling its surface as it passed. The strange, even light which had shone over all the scene ever since the children had stepped out at the hillside door had now grown paler: it was not now bright enough to distinguish more than can be seen by an autumn twilight. The air was fresh and clear, though not the least cold; the drooping forms of the low-hanging branches of the island trees gave the children a melancholy feeling when they glanced in that direction.

"I don't like this very much," said Jeanne. "It makes me sad, and I wanted to have fun."

"It must be sad for the poor swan if it's going to die," said Hugh. "But I don't mind this sort of sad feeling. I think it's rather nice. Ah! Jeanne, listen, there it is again. They must be going to begin."

"It" was a low sort of "call" which seemed to run round the shores of the lake like a preliminary note, and then completely died away. Instantly began from all sides the most curious music that Hugh and Jeanne had ever heard. It was croaking, but croaking in unison and regular time, and harsh as it was, there was a very strange charm about it—quite impossible to describe. It sounded pathetic at times, and at times monotonous, and yet inspiriting, like the beating of a drum; and the children listened to it with actual enjoyment. It went on for a good while, and then stopped as suddenly as it had begun; and then again, after some minutes of perfect silence, it recommenced in a low and regular chant—if such a word can be used for croaking—a steady, regular croak, croak, as if an immense number of harsh-sounding instruments were giving forth one note in such precise tune and measure that the harshness was softened and lost by the union of sound. It grew lower and lower, seeming almost to be about to die altogether away, when, from another direction—from the tree-shaded island in the centre of the lake—rose, low and faint at first, gathering strange strength as it mounted ever higher and higher, the song of the swan.

The children listened breathlessly and in perfect silence to the wonderful notes which fell on their ears—notes which no words of mine could describe, for in themselves they were words, telling of suffering and sorrow, of beautiful things and sad things, of strange fantastic dreams, of sunshine and flowers and summer days, of icy winds from the snow-clad hills, and days of dreariness and solitude. Each and all came in their turn; but, at the last, all melted, all grew rather, into one magnificent song of bliss and triumph, of joyful tenderness and brilliant hope, too pure and perfect to be imagined but in a dream. And as the last clear mellow notes fell on the children's ears, a sound of wings seemed to come with them, and gazing ever more intently towards the island they saw rising upwards the pure white snow-like bird—upwards and upwards, ever higher, till at last, with the sound of its own joyous song, it faded and melted into the opal radiance of the calm sky above.

For long the children gazed after it—a spot of light seemed to linger for some time in the sky just where it had disappeared—almost, to their fancy, as if the white swan was resting there, again to return to earth. But it was not so. Slowly, like the light of a dying star, the brightness faded; there was no longer a trace of the swan's radiant flight; again a soft low breeze, like a farewell sigh, fluttered across the lake, and the children withdrew their eyes from the sky and looked at each other.

"Jeanne!" said Hugh.

"Chéri!" said Jeanne.

"What was it? Was it not an angel, and not a swan?"

Jeanne shook her little head in perplexity.

"I don't know," she said. "It was wonderful. Did you hear all it told, Chéri?"

"Yes," said Hugh. "But no one could ever tell it again, Jeanne. It is a secret for us."

"And for the frogs," added Jeanne.

"And for the frogs," said Hugh.

"But," said Jeanne, "I thought the swan was going to die. *That* was not dying."

"Yes," said the queer croaking voice of the frog, suddenly reappearing on the edge of the boat; "yes, my children," he repeated, with a strange solemnity, "for such as the swan that *is* dying. And now once more—for you will never see me again, nor revisit this country—once again, my children, I bid you farewell."

He waved his hands in adieu, and hopped away.

"Chéri," said Jeanne, after a short silence, "I feel rather sad, and a very little sleepy. Do you think I might lie down a little—it is not the least cold—and take a tiny sleep? You might go to sleep too, if you like. I should think there will be time before we row back to the shore, only I do not know how we shall get the boat through the narrow part if the frogs have all gone. And no doubt Houpet and the others will be wondering why we are so long."

"We can whistle for Dudu again if we need," said Hugh. "He helped us very well the last time. I too am rather sleepy, Jeanne, but still I think I had better not go *quite* asleep. You lie down, and I'll just paddle on very slowly and softly for a little, and when you wake up we'll fix whether we should whistle or not."

Jeanne seemed to fall asleep in a moment when she lay down. Hugh paddled on quietly, as he had said, thinking dreamily of the queer things they had seen and heard in this nameless country inside the tapestry door. He did not feel troubled as to how they were to get back again; he had great faith in Dudu, and felt sure it would all come right. But gradually he too began to feel very sleepy; the dip of the oars and the sound of little Jeanne's regular breathing seemed to keep time together in a curious way. And at last the oars slipped from Hugh's hold; he lay down beside Jeanne, letting the boat drift; he was so *very* sleepy, he could keep up no more.

But after a minute or two when, not *quite* asleep, he lay listening to the soft breathing of the little girl, it seemed to him he heard still the gentle dip of the oars. The more he listened, the more sure he became that it was so, and at last his curiosity grew so great that it half overcame his drowsiness. He opened his eyes just enough to look up. Yes, he was right, the boat was gliding steadily along, the oars were doing their work, and who do you think were the rowers? Dudu on one side, Houpet on the other, rowing away as cleverly as if they had never done anything else in their lives, steadying themselves on one claw, rowing with the other. Hugh did not feel the least surprised; he smiled sleepily, and turned over quite satisfied.

"They'll take us safe back," he said to himself: and that was all he thought about it.

"Good-night, Chéri, good-night," was the next thing he heard, or remembered hearing.

Hugh half sat up and rubbed his eyes.

Where was he?

Not in the boat, there was no sound of oars, the light that met his gaze was not that of the strange country where Jeanne and he had had all these adventures, it was just clear ordinary moonlight; and as for where he was, he was lying on the floor of the tapestry room close to the part of the wall where stood, or hung, the castle with the long flight of steps, which Jeanne and he had so wished to enter. And from the other side of the tapestry—from inside the castle, one might almost say—came the voice he had heard in his sleep, the voice which seemed to have awakened him.

"Good-night, Chéri," it said, "good-night. I have gone home the other way."

"Jeanne, Jeanne, where are you? Wait!" cried Hugh, starting to his feet. But there was no reply.

Hugh looked all round. The room seemed just the same as usual, and if he had looked out of the window, though this he did not know, he would have seen the old raven on the terrace marching about, and, in his usual philosophical way, failing the sunshine, enjoying the moonlight; while down in the chickens' house, in the corner of the yard, Houpet and his friends were calmly roosting; fat little Nibble soundly sleeping in his cage, cuddled up in the hay; poor, placid Grignan reposing in his usual corner under the laurel bush. All these things Hugh would have seen, and would no doubt have wondered much at them. But though neither tired nor cold, he was still sleepy, very sleepy, so, after another stare all round, he decided that he would defer further inquiry till the morning, and in the meantime follow the advice of Jeanne's farewell "good-night."

And "after all," he said to himself, as he climbed up into his comfortable bed, "after all, bed is very nice, even though that little carriage was awfully jolly, and the boat almost better. What fun it will be to talk about it all to-morrow morning with Jeanne."

It was rather queer when to-morrow morning came—when he woke to find it had come, at least; it was rather queer to see everything looking just the same as on other to-morrow mornings. Hugh had not time to think very much about it, for it had been Marcelline's knock at the door that had wakened him, and she told him it was rather later than usual. Hugh, however, was so eager to see Jeanne and talk over with her their wonderful adventures that he needed no hurrying. But, to his surprise, when he got to Jeanne's room, where as usual their "little breakfast" was prepared for them on the table by the fire, Jeanne was seated on her low chair, drinking her coffee in her every-day manner, not the least different from what she always was, not in any particular hurry to see him, nor, apparently, with anything particular to say.

"Well, Chéri," she said, merrily, "you are rather late this morning. Have you slept well?"

Hugh looked at her; there was no mischief in her face; she simply meant what she said. In his astonishment, Hugh rubbed his eyes and then stared at her again.

"Jeanne," he said, quite bewildered.

"Well, Chéri," she repeated, "what is the matter?

How funny you look!" and in her turn Jeanne seemed surprised.

Hugh looked round; old Marcelline had left the room.

"Jeanne," he said, "it is so queer to see you just the same as usual, with nothing to say about it all."

"About all what?" said Jeanne, seemingly more and more puzzled.

"About our adventures—the drive in the carriage, with Houpet as coachman, and the stair down to the frog's country, and the frogs and the boat, and the concert, and O Jeanne! the song of the swan."

Jeanne opened wide her eyes.

"Chéri!" she said, "you've been dreaming all these funny things."

Hugh was so hurt and disappointed that he nearly began to cry.

"O Jeanne," he said, "it is very unkind to say that," and he turned away quite chilled and perplexed.

Jeanne ran after him and threw her arms round his neck.

"Chéri, Chéri," she said, "I didn't mean to vex you, but I *don't* understand."

Hugh looked into her dark eyes with his earnest blue ones.

"Jeanne," he said, "don't you remember *any* of it—don't you remember the trees changing their colours so prettily?—don't you remember the frogs' banquet?"

Jeanne stared at him so earnestly that she quite frowned.

"I think—I think," she said, and then she stopped. "When you say that of the trees, I think I did see rainbow colours all turning into each other. I think, Chéri, part of me was there and part not; can there be two of me, I wonder? But please, Chéri, don't ask me any more. It puzzles me so, and then perhaps I may say something to vex you. Let us play at our day games now, Chéri, and never mind about the other things. But if you go anywhere else like that, ask the fairies to take me too, for I always like to be with you, you know, Chéri."

So they kissed and made friends. But still it seemed very queer to Hugh. Till now Jeanne had always been eager to talk about the tapestry castle, and full of fancies about Dudu and Houpet and the rest of the animals, and anxious to hear Hugh's dreams. Now she seemed perfectly content with her every-day world, delighted with a new and beautiful china dinner-service which her godmother had sent her, and absorbed in cooking all manner of wonderful dishes for a grand dolls' feast, for which she was sending invitations to all her dolls, young and old, ugly and pretty, armless, footless, as were some, in the perfection of Parisian toilettes as were others. For she had, like most only daughters, an immense collection of dolls, though she was not as fond of them as many little girls.

"I thought you didn't much care for dolls. It was one of the things I liked you for at the first," said Hugh, in a slightly aggrieved tone of voice. Lessons were over, and the children were busy at the important business of cooking the feast. Hugh didn't mind the cooking; he had even submitted to a paper cap which Jeanne had constructed for him on the model of that of the "chef" downstairs; he found great consolation in the beating up an egg which Marcelline had got for them as a great treat, and immense satisfaction in watching the stewing, in one of Jeanne's toy pans on the nursery fire, of a preparation of squashed prunes, powdered chocolate, and bread crumbs, which was to represent a "ragout à la" —I really do not remember what.

"I thought you didn't care for dolls, Jeanne," Hugh repeated. "It would be ever so much nicer to have all the animals at our feast We could put them on chairs all round the table. That *would* be some fun."

"They wouldn't sit still one minute," said Jeanne. "How funny you are to think of such a thing, Chéri! Of course it would be fun if they *would,* but fancy Dudu and Grignan helping themselves with knives and forks like people."

Jeanne burst out laughing at the idea, and laughed so heartily that Hugh could not help laughing too. But all the same he said to himself,

"I'm sure Dudu and the others *could* sit at the table and behave like ladies and gentlemen if they chose. How *very* funny of Jeanne to forget about all the clever things they did! But it is no use saying any more to her. It would only make us quarrel. There must be two Jeannes, or else 'they,' whoever they are, make her forget on purpose."

And as Hugh, for all his fancifulness, was a good deal of a philosopher, he made up his mind to amuse himself happily with little Jeanne as she was. The feast was a great success. The dolls behaved irreproachably, with which their owner was rather inclined to twit Hugh, when, just at the end of the banquet, greatly to his satisfaction, a certain Mademoiselle Zéphyrine, a blonde with flaxen ringlets and turquoise blue eyes, suddenly toppled over, something having no doubt upset her equilibrium, and fell flat on her nose on the table.

"Ah!" cried Jeanne, greatly concerned, "my poor Zéphyrine has fainted," and, rushing forward to her assistance, worse results followed. Mesdames Lili and Joséphine, two middle-aged ladies somewhat the worse for wear, overcome by the distressing spectacle, *or* by the sleeve of Jeanne's dress as she leant across them, fell off their chairs too—one, like Zéphyrine, on to the table, the other on to the floor, dragging down with her the plateful of ragout in front of her, while her friend's sudden descent upon the table completed the general knockings over and spillings which Zéphyrine had begun.

"Oh dear! oh dear!" cried Jeanne; "all the chocolate ragout is spilt, and the whipped-up egg is mixed with the orange-juice soup. Oh dear! oh dear! and I thought we should have had the whole feast to eat up ourselves after the dolls had had enough."

"Yes," said Hugh, "that's what comes of having stupid sticks of dolls at your feasts. The *animals* wouldn't have behaved like that."

But, seeing that poor Jeanne was really in tears

at this unfortunate termination of her entertainment, he left off teasing her, and having succeeded in rescuing some remains of the good things, they sat down on the floor together and ate them up very amicably.

"I don't think I *do* care much for dolls," said Jeanne meditatively, when she had munched the last crumbs of the snipped-up almonds, which were supposed to represent some very marvellous dish. ("I like almonds terribly—don't you, Chéri?") she added, as a parenthesis. "No, I don't care for dolls. You are quite right about them; they *are* stupid, and you can't make fancies about them, because their faces always have the same silly look. I don't know what I like playing at best. O Marcelline!" she exclaimed, as the old nurse just then came into the room, "O Marcelline! *do* tell us a story; we are tired of playing."

"Does Monsieur Chéri, too, wish me tell him a story?" asked Marcelline, looking curiously at Hugh.

"Yes, of course," said Hugh. "Why do you look at me that funny way, Marcelline?"

"Why," said Marcelline, smiling, "I was thinking only that perhaps Monsieur finds so many stories in the tapestry that he would no longer care for my stupid little old tales."

Hugh did not answer. He was wondering to himself what Marcelline really meant; whether she knew of the wonders concealed behind the tapestry, or was only teasing him a little in the kind but queer way she sometimes did.

"Marcelline," he said suddenly at last, "I don't understand you."

"Do you understand yourself, my little Monsieur?" said Marcelline. "Do any of us understand ourselves? all the different selves that each of us is?"

"No," said Hugh, "I daresay we don't. It is very puzzling; it's all very puzzling."

"In the country where I lived when I was a little girl," began Marcelline, but Jeanne interrupted her.

"Have you never been there since, Marcelline?" she asked.

Marcelline smiled again her funny smile.

"Oh dear, yes," she said; "often, very often. I should not have been near so happy as I am if I had not often visited that country."

"Dear me," exclaimed Jeanne, "how very queer! I had no idea of that. You haven't been there for a great many years any way, Marcelline. I heard mamma telling a lady the other day that she never remembered your going away, not even for a day—never since she was born."

"Ah!" said Marcelline, "but, Mademoiselle, we don't always know what even those nearest us do. I might have gone to that country without your mamma knowing. Sometimes we are far away when those beside us think us close to them."

"Yes," said Hugh, looking up suddenly, "that is true, Marcelline."

What she said made him remember Dudu's remark about Jeanne the night before, that she was far, far away, and he began to feel that Marcelline understood much that she seldom alluded to.

But Jeanne took it up differently. She jumped on to Marcelline's knee and pretended to beat her.

"You naughty little old woman," she said; "you very naughty little old woman, to say things like that to puzzle me—just what you know I don't like. Go back to your own country, naughty old Marcelline; go back to your fairyland, or wherever it was you came from, if you are going to tease poor little Jeanne so."

"*Tease* you, Mademoiselle?" Marcelline repeated.

"Yes, tease me," insisted Jeanne. "You know I

hate people to go on about things I don't understand. Now you're to tell us a story at once, do you hear, Marcelline ? "

Hugh said nothing, but he looked up in Marcelline's face with his grave blue eyes, and the old woman smiled again. She seemed as if she was going to speak, when just then a servant came upstairs to say that Jeanne's mother wished the children to go downstairs to her for a little. Jeanne jumped up, delighted to welcome any change.

" You must keep the story for another day, Marcelline," she said, as she ran out of the room.

" I am getting too old to tell stories," said Marcelline, half to herself, half to Hugh, who was following his cousin more slowly. He stopped for a moment.

" Too old ? " he repeated.

" Yes, Monsieur Chéri, too old," the nurse replied. " The thoughts do not come so quickly as they once did, and the words, too, hobble along like lamesters on crutches."

" But," said Hugh, half timidly, " it is never—you would never, I mean, be too old to visit that country, where there are so many stories to be found ? "

" Perhaps not," said Marcelline, " but even if I found them, I might not be able to tell them. Go and look for them for yourself, Monsieur Chéri; you have not half seen the tapestry castle yet."

But when Hugh would have asked her more she would not reply, only smiled and shook her head. So the boy went slowly downstairs after Jeanne, wondering what old Marcelline could mean, half puzzled and half pleased.

"Only," he said to himself, "if I get into the castle, Jeanne really must come with me, especially if it is to hear stories."

CHAPTER VII.

WINGS AND CATS.

"And all their cattish gestures plainly spoke
They thought the affair they'd come upon no joke."
CHARLES LAMB.

SOME days went on, and nothing more was said by the children about the adventures which had so puzzled poor Hugh. After a while he seemed to lose the wish to talk about them to little Jeanne; or rather, he began to feel as if he could not, that the words would not come, or that if they did, they would not tell what he wanted. He thought about the strange things he had seen very often, but it was as if he had read of them rather than as if he had seen and heard them, or as if they had happened to some one else. Whenever he saw Dudu and Houpet and the rest of the pets, he looked at them at first in a half dreamy way, wondering if they too were puzzled about it all, or if, being really fairies, they did not find anything to puzzle them! The only person (for, after all, he could often not prevent himself from looking upon all the animals as persons)—the only person who he somehow felt sure *did* understand him, was Marcelline, and this was a great satisfaction. She said nothing; she almost never even smiled in what Jeanne called her "funny" way; but there was just a very tiny little undersound in the tone of her voice sometimes, a little wee smile in her eyes more than on her lips, that told Hugh that, fairy or no fairy, old Marcelline knew all about it, and it pleased him to think so.

One night when Hugh was warmly tucked up in bed Marcelline came in as usual before he went to sleep to put out his light.

"There's been no moonlight for a good while Marcelline, has there?" he said.

"No, Monsieur, there has not," said Marcelline.

"Will it be coming back soon?" asked Hugh.

"Do you like it so much, my child?" said the old nurse. She had a funny way of sometimes answering a question by asking another.

"Yes," said Hugh. "At least, of course when I'm fast asleep it doesn't matter to me if it's moonlight or not. But you know what I like it for, Marcelline, and you said the other day that I hadn't half seen the tapestry castle, and I want very much to see it, Marcelline, only I'd like Jeanne to be with me; for I don't think I could tell her well about the fairy things if she hadn't been with me. She didn't seem to understand the words, and I don't think I could get the right ones to tell, do you know, Marcelline?"

He half sat up in bed, resting his head on his elbow, which was leaning on the pillow, and looking up in the old woman's face with his earnest blue eyes. Marcelline shook her head slowly.

"No," she said, "you're right. The words wouldn't come, and if they did, it would be no use. You're older than Mademoiselle Jeanne, Monsieur Hugh, and it's different for her. But it doesn't matter—the days bring their own pleasures and interests, which the moonlight wouldn't suit. You wouldn't have cared for a dinner like what you have every day when you were listening to the song of the swan?"

"No, certainly not," said Hugh. "I see you do understand, Marcelline, better than anybody. It must be as I said; there must be two of me, and two of Jeanne, and two of you, and——"

"And two of everything," said Marcelline; "and

the great thing is to keep each of the twos in its right place."

She smiled now, right out, and was turning away with the light in her hand, when Hugh called after her,

"*Will* the moonlight nights come again soon, Marcelline? Do tell me. I'm sure you know."

"Have a little patience," said the old nurse, "you shall be told. Never fear."

And, a little inclined to be *im*patient, Hugh was nevertheless obliged to shut his eyes and go to sleep. There was no moonlight *that* night any way.

But not many nights after there came a great surprise.

Curiously enough Hugh had gone to sleep *that* night without any thought of tapestry adventures. He and Jeanne had been very merry indeed; they had been dressing up, and playing delightful tricks—such as tapping at the salon door, and on being told to come in, making their appearance like two very, very old peasants, hobbling along on sticks—Jeanne with a cap and little knitted shawl of Marcelline's, Hugh with a blouse and cotton nightcap, so that Jeanne's mother quite jumped at first sight of the quaint little figures. Then Jeanne dressed up like a fairy, and pretended to turn Hugh into a guinea-pig, and they got Nibble up into the nursery, and Hugh hid in a cupboard, and tried to make his voice sound as if it came from Nibble, and the effect of his ventriloquism was so comical that the children laughed till they actually rolled on the floor. And they had hardly got over the laughing—though Marcelline did her best to make them sit still for half an hour or so before going to bed—when it was time to say good-night and compose themselves to sleep.

"I shan't be able to go to sleep for ever so long," said Hugh; "I shall stay awake all the night, I believe."

"Oh no, you won't," said Marcelline, with a smile, as she went off with the light.

And strange to say, hardly had she shut the door when Hugh did fall asleep—soundly asleep. He knew no more about who he was, or where he was, or anything—he just slept as soundly as a little top, without dreaming or starting in the least, for—dear me, I don't know for how long!—any way it must have been for several hours, when—in the strange sudden way in which once or twice before it had happened to him to awake in this curious tapestry room, he opened his eyes as if startled by an electric shock, and gazed out before him, as much awake as if he had never been asleep in his life.

What had awakened him, and what did he see? He could hardly have told what had awakened him but for what he *now* saw and heard. A voice, a very well-known little voice, was speaking to him. "Chéri dear," it said, "Chéri, I have come for you. And see what I have got for you." And there before him stood little Jeanne—but Jeanne as he had never seen her before. She seemed all glistening and shining—her dress was of some kind of sparkling white, and round her waist was a lovely silver girdle—her sleeves too were looped up with silver bands, and, prettiest of all, two snow-white wings were fastened to her shoulders. She looked like a fairy queen, or like a silvery bird turned into a little girl. And in her hand she held another pair of wings exactly like her own.

Hugh gazed at her.

"Have you been dressing up?" he said, "and in the middle of the night? oh how funny! But O, Jeanne, how pretty you look!"

Jeanne laughed merrily. "Come, get up quick, then," she said, "and I'll make you pretty too. Only I can't promise you a head-dress like mine, Chéri."

She gave her head a little toss, which made Hugh look at it. And now he noticed that on it she wore something very funny indeed, which at first, being black—for Jeanne's hair, you know, was black too—had not caught his attention. At first he thought it was some kind of black silk hood or cap, such as he had seen worn by some of the peasants in Switzerland, but looking again—no, it was nothing of the kind—the head-dress had a head of its own, and as Hugh stared, it cocked it pertly on one side in a way Hugh would have known again anywhere. Yes, it was Dudu, sitting on Jeanne's smooth little head as comfortably as if he had always been intended to serve the purpose of a bonnet.

"Dudu!" exclaimed Hugh.

"Of course," said Jeanne. "You didn't suppose we could have gone without him, Chéri."

"Gone where?" said Hugh, quite sitting up in bed by this time, but still a good deal puzzled.

"Up into the tapestry castle," said Jeanne, "where we've been wishing so to go, though we had to wait for the moonlight, you know."

The word made Hugh glance towards the window, for, for the first time he began to wonder how it was his room was so bright. Yes, it was streaming in, in a beautiful flood, and the tapestry on the walls had taken again the lovely tints which by daylight were no longer visible.

Hugh sprang out of bed. "Are these for me?" he said, touching the wings which Jeanne held.

"Certainly," she replied. "Aren't they pretty? Much nicer than your wall-climbers, Chéri. I chose them. Turn round and let me put them on."

She slipped them over his head—they seemed to be fastened to a band, and in a moment they had fitted themselves perfectly into their place. They were so light that Hugh was hardly conscious of them, and yet he could move them about—backwards and forwards, swiftly or slowly, just as he chose—and as easily as he could move his arms. Hugh was extremely pleased with them, but he looked at his little night-gown with sudden dismay.

"You said you'd make me look pretty too, Jeanne," he observed. "I don't care for myself—boys never care about being grandly dressed—but I shall look rather funny beside you, shan't I?"

"Wait a minute," said Jeanne, "you're not ready yet. I'm going to powder you. Shut your eyes."

He did so, and therefore could not see what Jeanne did, but he felt a sort of soft puff fly all over him, and opening his eyes again at Jeanne's bidding, saw, to his amazement, that he too was now dressed in the same pretty shiny stuff as his little cousin. They looked just like two Christmas angels on the top of a frosted Twelfth Night cake.

"There now," said Jeanne, "aren't you pleased? You don't know how nice you look. Now, Dudu we're quite ready. Are we to fly up to the castle?"

Dudu nodded his wise head. Jeanne took Hugh's hand, and without Hugh's quite knowing how it was managed, they all flew up the wall together, and found themselves standing on the castle terrace. There was no light streaming out from the windows this time, and the peacocks were quite motionless at their post.

"Are they asleep?" said Hugh.

"Perhaps," said Dudu, speaking for the first time. "They lead a monotonous life, you see. But there is no occasion to disturb them."

They were standing just in front of the door, by which, the last time, Hugh had entered the long lighted-up passage. As they stood waiting, the door slowly opened, but to Hugh's great surprise the inside was perfectly different. A very large white-painted hall was revealed to them. The ceiling was arched, and looking up, it seemed so very high, that it gave one more the feeling of being the sky than the roof of a house. This great hall was perfectly empty, but yet it did not feel chilly, and a faint pleasant perfume stole through it, as if not far off sweet-scented flowers and plants were growing.

Hugh and Jeanne stood hand-in-hand and looked around them. The door by which they had entered had closed noiselessly, and when they turned to see the way by which they had come in, no sign of a door was there. In the panels of white wood which formed the walls, it was somehow concealed.

"How shall we ever get out again?" said Hugh.

But Jeanne only laughed.

"We needn't trouble about that," she said. "We got back all right the last time. What I want to know is what are we to do next? I see no way out of this hall, and though it's rather nice, it's not very amusing. Dudu, I wish you would sit still—you keep giving little juggles on my head that are very uncomfortable, and make me feel as if I had a hat on that was always tumbling off."

"I beg your pardon, Mademoiselle Jeanne," replied Dudu with great dignity. "You really do say such foolish things sometimes that it is impossible to restrain one's feelings altogether. No way out of this hall, do you say, when it is the entrance to everywhere?"

"But how are we to get to everywhere, or anywhere?" asked Jeanne.

"Really!" said Dudu, as if quite out of patience. "When you are running up and down the terrace, in your other life, you don't stand still at one end and say, 'Dudu, how am I to get to the other?' You move your feet, which were given you for the purpose. And in present circumstances, instead of your feet, you naturally——"

"Move our wings," cried Jeanne. "Oh, of course. We're to fly. But you see, Dudu, we're accustomed to having feet, and to running and walking with them, but having wings is something new."

Dudu still looked rather contemptuous, and Hugh gave a little pull to Jeanne's hand.

"Let's set off," he said.

"But where are we to go to?" asked Jeanne.

Dudu gave a little croak. "Really," he said again. "What am I here for?"

"Oh, to show us the way, of course," said Jeanne. "You're going to steer us, I suppose, on the top of my head. Well, we're quite ready."

Off they set. The flying this time was really quite a pleasure in itself, and the higher up they rose the easier and swifter it seemed to become. The hall was lighted from the roof—at least the light seemed to come down from among the arches so high up that their form was only vaguely seen. But whether it was daylight or what, the children did not know, and perhaps it did not occur to them to think. They just flew softly on, till suddenly Dudu veered to one side and stopped them in front of a low carved door with a step before it just large enough for them to stand on. They had not noticed this door before—the hall was so very large and the door in comparison so small, and the step before it had looked just like a little jutting-out ledge in the carving, till they were close to it.

"Don't turn round," said Dudu, "for fear it should make you giddy. Push the door and go in at once."

The children did so. The door yielded, and then immediately—they were such well-behaved doors in the tapestry palace—closed behind them. And what the children now saw was a small winding stair, the lowest steps of which were close to their feet.

"Here," said Dudu, "I will leave you. You can't go wrong."

He flew down from Jeanne's head as he spoke. Jeanne gave her head a little shake; she seemed not altogether sorry to be freed from her head-dress, for a head-dress with *feelings* is a somewhat uncomfortable affair.

"I don't mind you getting off my head, Dudu," she said. "But you might take a turn on Chéri's for a change. I think it's rather shabby of you to leave us already."

Hugh looked at Jeanne in surprise. He could not understand how it was that Jeanne ventured to speak so coolly to the raven—she who in their daylight life was so frightened of him that she would hardly go near him for fear he should turn her into a mouse, or in some other way bewitch her!

"I think it's very good-natured of Monsieur Dudu to have come with us so far," he said. "We could never have got into the tapestry castle at all but for him."

"No," said Dudu, "that you certainly wouldn't." But he didn't seem offended. "Good-bye," he said, "and if you're in any trouble remember the former arrangement. Whistle three times."

"Good-bye," said Hugh and Jeanne. But as they said it, their looks met each other in astonishment—

there was no Dudu there — he had already disappeared.

"What a queer way he has of going off all of a sudden," said Jeanne.

"And what are we to do now?" said Hugh.

"Go up the stairs, of course, till we find where they lead to," said Jeanne.

"It will be rather awkward with our wings," said Hugh. "The stair is so very narrow and twisting."

Jeanne made an exclamation.

"Wings!" she said. "Why, Chéri, your wings are gone!"

"And so are yours!" said Hugh.

Both the children stared at each other and turned round to look at their shoulders, as if they could hardly believe it.

"It's too bad," said Jeanne. "It's all Dudu."

"Never mind," said Hugh. "He wouldn't have taken them away if we had been going to need them again; and really, Jeanne, the more I think of it the more sure I am we could never have got up that stair with our wings on."

"Perhaps not," said Jeanne. "Any way *I* couldn't have got up it with Dudu on my head. But let's go on, Chéri. Are you frightened? I'm not a bit."

"I'm not, either," said Hugh. "Still, it's a very queer place. I wish Dudu, or Houpet, or some of them, had come with us!"

They set off on their climb up the steep spiral staircase. So narrow it was, that going hand-in-hand was out of the question.

"It's worse than the staircase down to the frogs' country," said Jeanne.

Hugh looked at her triumphantly.

There now, Jeanne, you *do* remember," he said. "I believe it was just pretence your saying you thought I had dreamt it all."

"No," said Jeanne, "it wasn't. You don't understand, Chéri. I'm moonlight Jeanne, now—when we were having the dolls' feast I was daylight Jeanne. And you know it's never moonlight in the day-time."

"Well, certainly, I *don't* understand," said Hugh. "And one thing particularly—how is it that in the moon-time you remember about the day-time, if in the day you forget all about the other."

"I don't exactly forget," said Jeanne, "but it spoils things to mix them together. And lots of things would be *quite* spoilt if you took them into the regular daylight. I fancy, too, one can see farther in the moonlight—one can see more ways."

She was standing at the foot of the stair, a step or two higher than Hugh, and the soft light, which still, in some mysterious way, seemed to come down from above—though, looking up the spiral stair, its top seemed lost in gloom—fell on her pretty little face. Her hair had fallen back over her shoulders and lay dark on her pure white shiny dress; there was a look in her eyes which Hugh had never noticed before, as if she could see a long way off. Hugh looked at her earnestly.

"Jeanne," he said, "you're a perfect puzzle. I do wonder whether you're half a fairy, or an angel, or a dream. I do hope you're not a dream when you're in the moonlight. But, oh dear, I cannot understand."

"Do leave off trying to understand, Chéri," said Jeanne, "and let us amuse ourselves. I always love *you*, Chéri, whatever I am, don't I?"

She turned towards him brightly, with such a merry smile on her face that Hugh could not help smiling too.

"Do let us go on quickly," she said; "I do so want to see where this stair goes to."

"Let me go first. I'm a boy, you know, and it's right I should go first in case of meeting anything that might frighten you," said Hugh.

So he stepped up in front of Jeanne, and they slowly made their way.

It was impossible to go fast. Never was there such a twisty little stair. Here and there, too, it got darker, so that they could only just find their way, step by step. And it really seemed as if they had climbed a very long way, when from above came faintly and softly the sound of a plaintive "mew." "Mew, mew," it said again, whoever the "it" was, and then stopped.

The children looked at each other.

"Cats!" they said at the same instant.

"It's just as well," said Hugh, "that none of the animals did come with us, as so many of them are birds."

Another step or two and the mystery was explained. They had reached the top of the turret stair; it led them into a little hall, all, like the great hall below, painted white. It looked perfectly pure and clean, as if it had only been painted the day before, and yet there was a curiously *old* look about it too, and a faint scent of dried rose leaves seemed to be in the air.

There was a door in this little hall, exactly opposite the top of the stair, and at each side of the door was an arm-chair, also all white, and with a white satin cushion instead of a seat. And on each of these chairs sat a most beautiful white cat. The only colour in the hall was the flash of their green eyes, as they turned them full on the two children.

Jeanne crept a little closer to Hugh. But there was no reason for fear. The cats were most amiably disposed.

"Mew!" said the one on the right-hand chair.

"Mew!" said the one on the left-hand chair.

Then they looked at each other for a moment, and at last, seeming to have made up their minds, each held out his right paw. Something in the way they did it reminded Hugh and Jeanne of Dudu when he stood on one leg, and stuck out the other like a walking-stick.

"Mew!" they said again, both together this time. And then in a clear, though rather mewey voice, the right-hand cat spoke to the children.

"Madame is expecting you," he said.

The children did not know what else to say, so they said, "Thank you."

"She has been waiting a good while," said the left-hand cat.

"I'm very sorry to have kept her waiting," said

Hugh, feeling Jeanne nudge him. "I hope she has not been waiting very long?"

"Oh no," said the right-hand cat, "not long; not above three hundred years."

Jeanne gave a start of astonishment.

"Three hundred——" "years," she was going to say, but the left-hand cat interrupted her.

"You are not to be surprised," he said, very hastily, and Jeanne could not quite make out if he was frightened or angry, or a little of both. "You must not *think* of being surprised. Nobody is ever surprised here."

"No one is ever surprised here," repeated the right-hand cat. "This is the Castle of Whiteness, you know. You are sure you have nothing coloured about you?" he added, anxiously.

Instinctively both the children put their hands up to their heads.

"Only our hair," they said.

"Mine's light-brown, you see," said Hugh.

"And mine's bl——" Jeanne was saying, but the cats, both speaking together this time, stopped her with a squeal of horror.

"Oh, oh, oh!" they said. "Where are your manners? You must never mention such a word. Your hair, Mademoiselle, is *shadowy*. That is the proper expression."

Jeanne was annoyed, and did not speak. Hugh felt himself bound to defend her from the charge of bad manners.

"You needn't be so sharp," he said to the cats; "your eyes are as green as they can be."

"Green doesn't count," said the right-hand cat, coolly.

"And how were we to know that?" said Hugh.

"I don't know," said the left-hand cat.

"Well, but can't you be sensible?" said Hugh, who didn't feel inclined to give in to two cats.

"Perhaps we might be if we tried," said the right-hand cat. "But——"

A sudden sound interrupted him. It was as if some one had moved a piece of furniture with squeaking castors.

"Madame's turning her wheel," said the left-hand cat. "Now's the time."

Both cats got down from their chairs, and each, standing on their hind legs, proceeded to open his side of the door between the chairs—or "doors" I should almost say, for it was a double-hinged one, opening in the middle, and the funny thing about it was that one side opened outwards, and the other inwards, so that at first, unless you were standing just exactly in the middle, you did not see very clearly into the inside.

CHAPTER VIII.

"THE BROWN BULL OF NORROWA."

"Delicate, strong, and white,
Hurrah for the magic thread!
The warp and the woof come right."

CHILD WORLD.

THEY were not to be surprised! Both the children remembered that, and yet it was a little difficult to avoid being so.

At first all they saw was just another white room, a small one, and with a curious pointed window in one corner. But when the doors were fully opened there was more to be seen. In the first place, at the opposite corner, was a second window exactly like the other, and in front of this window a spinning-wheel was placed, and before this spinning-wheel sat, on a white chair, a white-haired lady.

She was spinning busily. She did not look up as the children came in. She seemed quite absorbed in her work. So the children stood and gazed at her, and the cats stood quietly in front, the right-hand one before Hugh, the left-hand one before Jeanne, not seeming, of course, the least surprised. Whether I should call the white-haired lady an "old" lady oı not, I really do not know. No doubt she was old, as we count old, but yet, except for her hair, she did not look so. She was very small, and she was dressed entirely in white, and her hands were the prettiest little things you ever saw. But as she did not look up, Hugh and Jeanne could not at first judge of her face. They stood staring at her for some minutes without speaking. At last, as they were not allowed to be surprised, and indeed felt afraid of being reproached with bad manners by the cats if they made any remarks at all, it began, especially for Jeanne, to grow rather stupid.

She gave Hugh a little tug.

"Won't you speak to her?" she whispered, very, *very* softly.

Instantly both cats lifted their right paws.

"You see," replied Hugh, looking at Jeanne reproachfully, "they're getting angry."

On this the cats wheeled right round and looked at the children.

"I don't care," said Jeanne, working herself up.

"I don't care. It's not our fault. They said she was waiting for us, and they made us come in."

"'*She* is the cat,' so I've been told," said a soft voice suddenly. And 'don't care;' something was once spun about 'don't care,' I think."

Immediately the two cats threw themselves on the ground, apparently in an agony of grief.

"*She* the cat," they cried. "Oh, what presumption! And who said 'don't care'? Oh dear! oh dear! who would have thought of such a thing?"

The lady lifted her head, and looked at the cats and the children. There was a curious expression on her face, as if she had just awakened. Her eyes were very soft blue, softer and dreamier than Hugh's, and her mouth, even while it smiled, had a rather sad look. But the look of her whole face was very —I can't find a very good word for it. It seemed to ask you questions, and yet to know more about you than you did yourself. It was impossible not to keep looking at her once you had begun.

"Hush, cats," were the next words she said. "Don't be silly; it's nearly as bad as being surprised."

Immediately the cats sat up in their places again, as quiet and dignified as if they had not been at all put about, and Jeanne glanced at Hugh as much as to say, "Aren't you glad she has put them down a little?"

Then the lady looked over the cats to the children.

"It is quite ready," she said; "the threads are all straight."

What could they say? They had not the least idea what she meant, and they were afraid of asking. Evidently the white lady was of the same opinion as the cats as to the rudeness of being surprised; very probably asking questions would be considered still ruder.

Jeanne was the first to pick up courage.

"Madame," she said, "I don't mean to be rude, but I *am* so thirsty. It's with flying, I think, for we're not accustomed to it."

"Why did you not say so before?" said the lady. "I can give you anything you want. It has all been ready a long time. Will you have snow water or milk?"

"Milk, please," said Jeanne.

The lady looked at the cats.

"Fetch it," she said quietly. The cats trotted off, they opened the door as before, but left it open this time, and in another moment they returned, carrying between them a white china tray, on which were two cups of beautiful rich-looking milk. They handed them to the children, who each took one and drank it with great satisfaction. Then the cats took away the cups and tray, and returned and sat down as before.

The lady smiled at the children.

"Now," she said, "are you ready?"

She had been so kind about the milk that Hugh this time took courage.

"We are *very* sorry," he said, "but we really don't understand what it is you would like us to do."

"Do?" said the lady. "Why, you have nothing to do but to listen. Isn't that what you came for? To hear some of the stories I spin?"

The children opened their eyes—with pleasure it is to be supposed rather than surprise—for the white lady did not seem at all annoyed.

"Oh!" said they, both at once. "Is *that* what you're spinning? Stories!"

"Of course," said the lady. "Where did you think they all come from?—all the stories down there?" She pointed downwards in the direction of the stair and the great hall. "Why, here I have been for—no, it would frighten you to tell you how long, by your counting, I have been up here at my spinning. I spin the round of the clock at this window, then I turn my wheel—to get the light, you see—and spin the round again at the other. If you saw the tangle it comes to me in! And the threads I send down! It is not *often* such little people as you come up here themselves, but it does happen sometimes. And there is plenty ready for you—all ready for the wheel."

"How wonderful!" said Hugh. "And oh!" he exclaimed, "I suppose sometimes the threads get twisted again when you have to send them down such a long way, and that's how stories get muddled sometimes."

"Just so," said the white lady. "My story threads need gentle handling, and sometimes people seize them roughly and tear and soil them, and then of course they are no longer pretty. But listen now. What will you have? The first in the wheel is a very, very old fairy story. I span it for your great-great-grandmothers; shall I spin it again for you?"

"Oh, please," said both children at once.

"Then sit down on the floor and lean your heads against my knees," said the lady. "Shut your eyes and listen. That is all you have to do. Never mind the cats, they will be quite quiet."

STORY SPINNING.—p. 141.

Hugh and Jeanne did as she told them. They leaned their heads, the smooth black one of the little girl, the fair-haired curly one of the boy, on the lady's white robe. You can hardly imagine how soft and pleasant it was to the touch. A half-sleepy feeling came over them; they shut their eyes and did not feel inclined to open them again. But they did not really go to sleep; the fairy lady began to work the wheel, and through the soft whirr came the sound of a voice—whether it was the voice of the lady or of the wheel they could not tell. And this was the old, old story the wheel spun for them.

"Listen, children," it began.

"We are listening," said Jeanne, rather testily. "You needn't say that again."

"Hush, Jeanne," said Hugh; "you'll stop the story if you're not quiet."

"Listen, children," said the voice again. And Jeanne was quite quiet.

"Once on a time—a very long time ago—in a beautiful castle there lived a beautiful Princess. She was young and sweet and very fair to see. And she was the only child of her parents, who thought nothing too rare or too good for her. At her birth all the fairies had given her valuable gifts—no evil wishes had been breathed over her cradle. Only the fairy who had endowed her with good sense and ready wit had dropped certain words, which had left some anxiety in the minds of her parents.

"'She will need my gifts,' the fairy had said. 'If she uses them well, they and these golden balls will stand her in good need.

"And as she kissed the baby she left by her pillow three lovely golden balls, at which, as soon as the little creature saw them, she smiled with pleasure, and held out her tiny hands to catch them.

"They were of course balls of fairy make—they were small enough for the little Princess at first to hold in her baby hands, but as she grew they grew, till, when she had reached her sixteenth year, they were the size of an orange. They were golden, but yet neither hard nor heavy, and nothing had power to dint or stain them. And all through her babyhood and childhood, and on into her girlhood, they were the Princess's favourite toy. They were never away from her, and by the time she had grown to be a tall and beautiful girl, with constant practice she had learnt to catch them as cleverly as an Indian juggler. She could whiz them all three in the air at a time, and never let one drop to the ground. And all the people about grew used to seeing their pretty Princess, as she wandered through the gardens and woods near the castle, throwing her balls in the air as she walked, and catching them again without the slightest effort.

"And remembering the words of the fairy who had given them, naturally her father and mother were pleased to see her love for the magic gift, and every one about the palace was forbidden to laugh at her, or to say that it was babyish for a tall Princess to play so much with a toy that had amused her as an infant.

"She was not a silly Princess at all. She was clever at learning, and liked it, and she was sensible and quick-witted and very brave. So no one was inclined to laugh at her pretty play, even if they had not been forbidden to do so. And she was so kind-hearted and merry, that if ever in her rambles she met any little children who stared at her balls with wondering eyes, she would make her ladies stop, while she threw the balls up in the air, higher and yet higher, ever catching them again as they flew back, and laughed with pleasure to see the little creatures' delight in her skill.

"She was such a happy Princess that the bright balls seemed like herself—ready to catch every ray of sunshine and make it prisoner. And till she had reached her sixteenth year no cloud had come over her brightness. About this time she noticed that the king, her father, began to look anxious and grave, and messengers often came in haste to see him from far-off parts of his kingdom. And once or twice she overheard words dropped which she could not understand, except that it was evident some misfortune was at hand. But in their desire to save their daughter all sorrow, the king and queen had given orders that the trouble which had come to the country was not to be told her; so the Princess could find out nothing even by questioning her ladies or her old nurse, who hitherto had never refused to tell her anything she wanted to know.

"One day when she was walking about the gardens, playing as usual with her golden balls, she came upon a young girl half hidden among the shrubs, crying bitterly. The Princess stopped at once to ask her what was the matter, but the girl only shook her head and went on weeping, refusing to answer.

"'I dare not tell you, Princess,' she said. 'I dare not. You are good and kind, and I do not blame you for my misfortunes. If you knew all, you would pity me.'

"And that was all she would say.

"She was a pretty girl, about the same age and height as the Princess, and the Princess, after speaking to her, remembered that she had sometimes seen her before.

"'You are the daughter of the gardener, are you not?' she inquired.

"'Yes,' said the girl. 'My father is the king's gardener. But I have been away with my grandmother. They only sent for me yesterday to come home—and—and—oh, I was to have been married next week to a young shepherd, who has loved me since my childhood!'

"And with this the girl burst into fresh weeping, but not another word would she say.

"Just then the Princess's governess, who had been a little behind—for sometimes in playing with her balls the Princess ran on faster—came up to where the two young girls were talking together. When the governess saw who the Princess's companion was she seemed uneasy.

"'What has she been saying to you, Princess?' she asked eagerly. 'It is the gardener's daughter, I see.'

"'Yes,' said the Princess. 'She is the gardener's

daughter, and she is in some great trouble. That is all I know, for she will tell me nothing but that she was to have been married next week, and then she weeps. I wish I knew what her sorrow is, for, perhaps, I could be of use to her. I would give her all my money if it would do her any good,' and the Princess looked ready to cry herself. But the girl only shook her head. 'No Princess,' she said; 'it would do me no good. It is not your fault; but oh, it is very hard on me!'

"The governess seemed very frightened and spoke sharply to the girl, reproving her for annoying the Princess with her distress. The Princess was surprised, for all her ladies hitherto had, by the king and queen's desire, encouraged her to be kind and sympathising to those in trouble, and to do all she could to console them. But as she had also been taught to be very obedient, she made no remonstrance when her governess desired her to leave the girl and return to the castle. But all that day the Princess remained silent and depressed. It was the first time a shadow had come near her happiness.

"The next morning when she awoke the sun was shining brilliantly. It was a most lovely spring day. The Princess's happy spirits seemed all to have returned. She said to herself that she would confide to the queen her mother her concern about the poor girl that she had seen, and no doubt the queen would devise some way of helping her. And the thought made her feel so light-hearted that she told her attendants to fetch her a beautiful white dress trimmed with silver, which had been made for her but the day before. To her surprise the maidens looked at each other in confusion. At last one replied that the queen had not been pleased with the dress and had sent it away, but that a still more beautiful one trimmed with gold should be ready by that evening. The Princess was perplexed; she was not so silly as to care about the dress, but it seemed to her very strange that her mother should not admire what she had thought so lovely a robe. But still more surprised was she at a message which was brought to her, as soon as she was dressed, from the king and queen, desiring her to remain in her own rooms the whole of that day without going out, for a reason that should afterwards be explained to her. She made no objection, as she was submissive and obedient to her parents' wishes, but she found it strange and sad to spend that beautiful spring day shut up in her rooms, more especially as in her favourite boudoir, a turret chamber which overlooked the castle courtyard, she found the curtains drawn closely, as if it were night, and was told by her governess that this too was by the king's orders; the Princess was requested not to look out of the windows. She grew at this a little impatient.

"'I am willing to obey my parents,' she said, but I would fain they trusted me, for I am no longer a child. Some misfortune is threatening us, I feel, and it is concealed from me, as if I could be happy or at rest if sorrow is hanging over my dear parents or the nation.'

"But no explanation was given to her, and all that day she sat in her darkened chamber playing sadly with her golden balls and thinking deeply to herself about the mystery. And towards the middle of the day sounds of excitement reached her from the courtyard beneath. There seemed a running to and fro, a noise of horses and of heavy feet, and now and then faint sounds of weeping.

"'Goes the king a hunting to-day?' she asked her ladies. 'And whose weeping is it I hear?'

"But the ladies only shook their heads without speaking.

"By the evening all seemed quiet. The Princess

was desired to join her parents as usual, and the white and golden robe was brought to her to wear. She put it on with pleasure, and said to herself there could after all be no terrible misfortune at hand, for if so there would not be the signs of rejoicing she observed as she passed through the palace. And never had her parents been more tender and loving. They seemed to look at her as if never before they had known how they treasured her, and the Princess was so touched by these proofs of their affection that she could not make up her mind to trouble them by asking questions which they might not wish to answer.

"The next day everything went on as usual in the palace, and it seemed to the Princess that there was a general feeling as if some great danger was safely passed. But this happiness did not last long; about three days later, again a messenger, dusty and wearied with riding fast and hard, made his appearance at the castle; and faces grew gloomy, and the king and queen were evidently overwhelmed with grief. Yet nothing was told to the Princess.

"She wandered out about the gardens and castle grounds, playing as usual with her balls, but wondering sadly what meant this mysterious trouble. And as she was passing the poultry-yard, she heard a sound which seemed to suit her thoughts — some one was crying sadly. The Princess turned to see who it was. This time too it was a young girl about her own age, a girl whom she knew very well by sight, for she was the daughter of the queen's hen-wife, and the Princess had often seen her driving the flocks of turkeys or geese to their fields, or feeding the pretty cocks and hens which the queen took great pride in.

"'What is the matter, Bruna?' said the Princess, leaning over the gate. 'Have the rats eaten any of the little chickens, or has your mother been scolding you for breaking some eggs?'

"'Neither, Princess,' said the girl among her sobs. 'The chickens are never eaten, and my mother seldom scolds me. My trouble is far worse than that, but I dare not tell it to you—to you of all people in the world.'

"And the Princess's governess, who just then came up, looked again very frightened and uneasy.

"'Princess, Princess,' she said, 'what a habit you are getting of talking to all these foolish girls. Come back to the palace at once with me.'

"'I have often talked to Bruna before,' said the

Princess gently, 'and I never was blamed for doing so. She is a pretty girl, and I have known her all my life. Some one said she was betrothed to one of my father's huntsmen, and I would like to ask if it is true. Perhaps they are too poor to marry, and it may be for that she is weeping.'

"Bruna heard what the Princess said, and wept still more violently. 'Ah, yes, it is true!' she said, 'but never, never shall I now be married to him.'

"But the Princess's governess would not let her wait to ask more. She hurried her back to the castle, and the Princess—more sure than ever that some mysterious trouble was in question—could get no explanation.

"She did not see the king and queen that night, and the next morning a strange thing happened—her white and golden robe was missing. And all that her attendants could tell her was that it had been taken away by the queen's orders.

"'Then,' said the Princess, 'there is some sad trouble afloat which is hidden from me.'

"And when she went to her turret room, and found, as before, that the windows were all closed, so that she could not see out, she sat down and cried with distress and anxiety.

"And, again, about mid-day, the same confused noises were to be heard. A sound of horses and people moving about in the courtyard, a tramping of heavy feet, and through all a faint and smothered weeping. The Princess could bear her anxiety no longer. She drew back the curtains, and unfastened the shutters, and leaned out. From her window she could clearly see the courtyard. It was, as she suspected, filled with people; rows of soldiers on horseback lined the sides, and in front, on the steps, the king and queen were standing looking at a strange object. It was an enormous bull: never had the Princess seen such a bull. He was dark brown in colour, and pawed the ground in front of him impatiently, and on his back was seated a young girl whom the Princess gazed at with astonishment. She really thought for a moment it was herself, and that she was dreaming! For the girl was dressed in the Princess's own white and golden robe, and her face could not be seen, for it was covered with a thick veil, and numbers of women and servants standing about were weeping bitterly. And so, evidently, was the girl herself. Then the great bull gave another impatient toss, the girl seized his horns to keep herself from falling, and off he set, with a terrible rush;

and a great shout, half of fear, half of rejoicing, as seeing him go, rose from the people about.

"Just at this moment the Princess heard some one approaching her room. She hastily drew the curtains, and sat down playing with her balls, as if she had seen nothing.

"She said not a word to any one, but she had her own thoughts, and that evening she was sent for to her father and mother, who, as usual, received her with caresses and every sign of the tenderest affection. And several days passed quietly, but still the Princess had her own thoughts.

"And one evening when she was sitting with her mother, suddenly the king entered the room in the greatest trouble, and not seeing the Princess, for it was dusk, he exclaimed,

"'It has failed again. The monster is not to be deceived. He vows he will not cease his ravages till he gets the real Princess, our beloved daughter. He has appeared again, and is more infuriated than ever, tearing up trees by the roots, destroying the people's houses, tramping over their fields, and half killing all the country with terror. What is to be done? The people say they can endure it no longer. The girl Bruna was found bruised and bleeding by the wayside a long way from this, and she gives the same account as the gardener's daughter of the monster's rage at finding he had been deceived.'

"The queen had tried to prevent the king's relating all this, but he was too excited to notice her hints, and, indeed, after the first few words, the Princess had heard enough. She started from her seat and came forward. And when he saw her, the king threw up his hands in despair. But the Princess said quietly, 'Father, you must tell me the whole.'

"So they had to tell her the whole. For many weeks past the terrible monster she had seen in the courtyard had been filling the country with fear. He had suddenly appeared at a distant part of the kingdom—having come, it was said, from a country over the sea named 'Norrowa'—and had laid it waste, for though he did not actually kill or devour, he tore down trees, trampled crops, and terrified every one that came in his way, as the king had said. And when begged to have mercy and to return to his own country, he roared out with a voice between the voice of a man and the bellow of a bull, that he would leave them in peace once the king gave him his daughter in marriage.

"Messenger after messenger had been sent to the

palace to entreat for assistance. Soldiers in numbers had been despatched to seize the monster and imprison him. But it was no use—he was not to be caught. Nothing would content him but the promise of the Princess; and as it was of course plain that he was not a common bull, but a creature endowed with magical power, the country-people's fear of him was unbounded. They threatened to rise in revolution unless some means were found of ridding them of their terrible visitor. Then the king called together the wisest of his counsellors, and finding force of no avail, they determined to try cunning. The giving the Princess was not to be thought of, but a pretty girl about her age and size—the gardener's daughter, the same whom the Princess had found weeping over her fate—was chosen, dressed in one of her royal mistress's beautiful robes, and a message sent to the bull that his request was to be granted. He came. All round, the castle was protected by soldiers, though they well knew their power against him was nothing. The king and queen, feigning to weep over the loss of their daughter, themselves presented to him the false Princess.

"She was mounted on his back, and off he rushed with her—up hill, down dale, by rocky ground and smooth, across rivers and through forests he rushed, said the girl, faster and faster, till at last, as evening fell, he came to a stand and spoke to her for the first time.

"'What time of day must it be by this, king's daughter?' he said.

"The girl considered for a moment. Then, forgetting her pretended position, she replied thoughtlessly,

"'It must be getting late. About the time that my father gathers the flowers to adorn the king's and queen's supper table.'

"'Throw thee once, throw thee twice, throw thee *thrice*,' roared the bull, each time shaking the girl roughly, and the last time flinging her off his back. 'Shame on thee, gardener's daughter, and thou wouldst call thyself a true Princess.'

"And with that he left her bruised and frightened out of her wits on the ground, and rushed off by himself whither she knew not. And it was not till two days later that the unfortunate gardener's daughter found her way home, glad enough, one may be sure, to be again there in safety.

"In the meantime the ravages and terrors caused by the terrible bull had begun again, and, as before, messengers came incessantly to the king entreating him to find some means of protecting his unfortunate subjects. And the king and queen were half beside themselves with anxiety. Only one thing they were determined on—nothing must be told to the Princess.

CHAPTER IX.

THE BROWN BULL—(*Continued*).

"And she
Told them an old-world history."
MATTHEW ARNOLD.

"'SHE is so courageous,' said the queen, 'there is no knowing what she might not do.'

"'She is so kind-hearted,' said the king; 'she might imagine it her duty to sacrifice herself to our people.'

"And the poor king and queen wept copiously at the mere thought, and all the ladies and attendants of the Princess were ordered on no account to let a breath of the terrible story be heard by her. Yet, after all, it so happened that her suspicions were aroused afresh by the sight this time of the weeping Bruna. For nothing else could be suggested than again to try to deceive the monster; and Bruna, a still prettier girl than the gardener's daughter, was this time chosen to represent the Princess. But all happened as before. The brown bull rushed off with his prize, the whole day the unfortunate Bruna was shaken on his back, and again, as night began to fall, he stopped at the same spot.

"'What time must it be by this, king's daughter?' he asked.

"Foolish Bruna, thankful to have a moment's rest, answered hastily,

"'O brown bull, it must be getting late, and I am sorely tired. It must be about the time that my mother takes all the eggs that have been laid in the day to the king's kitchen.'

"'Throw thee once, throw thee twice, throw thee *thrice*,' roared the bull, each time shaking the henwife's daughter roughly, at the end flinging her to the ground. 'Shame on thee, thou henwife's daughter, to call thyself a true Princess.'

"And with that off he rushed, furious, and from that day the ravages and the terrors began again, and Bruna found her way home, bruised and weeping, to tell her story.

"This was the tale now related to the Princess, and as she listened a strange look of determination and courage came over her face.

"'There is but one thing to be done,' she said.

'It is childish to attempt to deceive a creature who is evidently not what he seems. Let me go myself, my parents. Trust me to do my best. And, at worst, if I perish, it will be in a good cause. Better it should be so than that our people should be driven from their homes, the whole country devastated, and all its happiness destroyed.'

"The king and queen had no answer to give but their tears. But the Princess remained firm, and they found themselves obliged to do as she directed. A messenger was sent to the monster to inform him, for the third time, that his terms were to be agreed to, and the rest of the day was spent in the palace in weeping and lamentation.

"Only, strange to say, the Princess shed no tears. She seemed as cheerful as usual; she played with her golden balls, and endeavoured to comfort her sorrowful parents, and was so brave and hopeful that in spite of themselves the poor king and queen could not help feeling a little comforted.

"'It is a good sign that she has never left off playing with her balls,' they said to each other. 'Who knows but what the fairy's prediction may be true, and that in some way the balls may be the means of saving her?'

"'They and my wits,' said the Princess, laughing, for she had often been told of the fairy's saying.

"And the king and queen and all the ladies and gentlemen of the court looked at her in astonishment, admiring her courage, but marvelling at her having the spirit to laugh at such a moment.

"The next morning, at the usual time, the terrible visitor made his appearance. He came slowly up to the castle courtyard and stood at the great entrance, tossing his enormous head with impatience. But he was not kept waiting long; the doors were flung open, and at the top of the flight of steps leading down from them appeared the young Princess, pale but resolute, her fair hair floating over her shoulders, her golden balls flashing as she slowly walked down the steps, tossing them as she went. And, unlike the false princesses, she was dressed entirely in black, without a single jewel or ornament of any kind—nothing but her balls, and her hair caught the sunlight as she passed. There were no soldiers this time, no crowd of weeping friends; the grief of the king and queen was now too real to be shown, and the Princess had asked that there should be no one to see her go.

"The brown bull stood still as a lamb for her to

mount, and then at a gentle pace he set off. The Princess had no need to catch hold of his horns to keep herself from falling, his step was so even. And all along as she rode she threw her balls up softly in the air, catching them as they fell. But the brown bull spoke not a word.

"On and on they went; the sun rose high in the heavens and poured down on the girl's uncovered head the full heat of his rays. But just as she began to feel it painfully, they entered a forest, where the green shade of the summer trees made a pleasant shelter. And when they came out from the forest again on the other side the sun was declining; before long he had sunk below the horizon, evening was at hand. And as before, the brown bull stopped.

"'King's daughter,' he said, in a voice so gentle, though deep, that the Princess started with surprise, 'what hour must it be by this? Tell me, king's daughter, I pray.'

"'Brown bull,' replied the Princess, without a moment's hesitation, for those who have nothing to conceal are fearless and ready; 'brown bull, it is getting late. By now must the king and queen, my father and mother, be sitting down to their solitary supper and thinking of me, for at this hour I was used

THE BROWN BULL OF NORROWA.—p. 162.

to hasten to them, throwing my pretty balls as I went.'

"'I thank thee, thou true Princess,' said the bull in the same tone, and he hastened on.

"And ere long the night fell, and the poor Princess was so tired and sleepy, that without knowing it her pretty head drooped lower and lower, and at last she lay fast asleep on the bull's broad back, her fair head resting between his horns.

"She slept so soundly that she did not notice when he stopped, only she had a strange dream. Some one lifted her gently and laid her on a couch, it seemed to her, and a kind voice whispered in her ear, 'Good-night, my fair Princess.'

"But it must have been a dream, she said to herself. How could a bull have arms to lift her, or how could a rough, ferocious creature like him be so gentle and kind? It must have been a dream, for when she awoke she saw the great monster standing beside her on his four legs as usual; yet it was strange, for she found herself lying on a delicious mossy couch, and the softest and driest moss had been gathered together for a pillow, and beside her a cup of fresh milk and a cake of oaten bread were lying for her breakfast. How had all this been done for her? she asked herself, as she ate with a very good appetite, for she had had no food since the morning before. She began to think the bull not so bad after all, and to wonder if it was to Fairyland he was going to take her. And as she thought this to herself she threw her balls, which were lying beside her, up into the air, and the morning sun caught their sparkle and seemed to send it dancing back again on to her bright fair hair. And a sudden fancy seized her.

"'Catch,' she said to the bull, throwing a ball at him as she spoke. He tossed his head, and to her surprise the ball was caught on one of his horns.

"'Catch,' she said again, and he had caught the second.

"'Catch,' a third time. The great creature caught it in his mouth like a dog, and brought it gently to the Princess and laid it at her feet. She took it and half timidly stroked his head; and no one who had seen the soft pathetic look which crept into his large round eyes would have believed in his being the cruel monster he had been described. He did not speak, he seemed without the power to do so now, but by signs he made the Princess understand it was time to continue their journey, and she mounted his back as before.

"All that day the bull travelled on, but the Princess was now getting accustomed to her strange steed, and felt less tired and frightened. And when the sun grew hot the bull was sure to find a sheltered path, where the trees shaded her from the glare, and when the road was rough he went the more slowly, that she should not be shaken.

"Late in the evening the Princess heard a far-off rushing sound, that as they went seemed to grow louder and louder.

"'What is that, brown bull?' she asked, feeling somehow a little frightened.

"The brown bull raised his head and looked round him. Yes, the sun had sunk, he might speak. And in the same deep voice he answered,

"'The sea, king's daughter, the sea that is to bear you and me to my country of Norrowa.'

"'And how shall we cross it, brown bull?' she said.

"'Have no fear," he replied. 'Lay down your head and shut your eyes, and no harm will come near you.'

"The Princess did as he bade her. She heard the roar of the waves come nearer and nearer, a cold wind blew over her face, and she felt at last that her huge steed had plunged into the water, for it splashed on to her hand, which was hanging downwards, and then she heard him, with a gasp and a snort, strike out boldly. The Princess drew herself up on the bull's back as closely as she could; she had no wish to get wet. But she was not frightened. She grew accustomed to the motion of her great steed's swimming, and as she kept her eyes fast shut she did not see how near she was to the water, and felt as if in a peaceful dream. And after a while the feeling became reality, for she fell fast asleep and dreamt she was in her little turret chamber, listening to the wind softly blowing through the casement.

"When she awoke she was alone. She was lying on a couch, but this time not of moss, but of the richest and softest silk. She rubbed her eyes and looked about her. Was she in her father's castle? Had her youth and her courage softened the monster's heart, and made him carry her back again to her happy home? For a moment she thought it must be so; but no, when she looked again, none of the rooms in her old home were so beautiful as this one where she found herself. Not even her mother's great saloon, which she had always thought so magnificent, was to be compared with it. It was not very large, but it was more like Fairyland than anything she had ever dreamt of. The loveliest flowers were trained against the walls, here and there fountains of delicately scented waters refreshed the air, the floor was covered with carpets of the richest hues and the softest texture. There were birds singing among the flowers, gold and silver fish sporting in the marble basins—it was a perfect fairy's bower. The Princess sat up and looked about her. There was no one to be seen, not a sound but the dropping of the fountains and the soft chatter of the birds. The Princess admired it all exceedingly, but she was very hungry, and as her long sleep had completely refreshed her, she felt no longer inclined to lie still. So she crossed the room to where a curtain was hanging, which she thought perhaps concealed a door. She drew aside the curtain, the door behind was already open; she found herself in a second room, almost as beautiful as the first, and lighted in the same way with coloured lamps hanging from the roof. And to her great delight, before her was a table already laid for supper with every kind of delicious fruit and bread, and cakes, and everything that a young Princess could desire. She was so hungry that she at once sat down to the table, and then she perceived to her surprise that it was laid for two!

"'Can the bull be coming to sup with me?' she

said to herself, half laughing at the idea. And she added aloud, 'Come if you like, Mr. Bull; I find your house very pretty, and I thank you for your hospitality.'

"And as she said the words, a voice which somehow seemed familiar to her, replied,

"'I thank you, gracious Princess, for your permission. Without it I could not have entered your presence as I do now,' and looking up, she saw, coming in by another door that she had not noticed, a most unexpected visitor.

"It was not the bull, it was a young Prince such as our pretty Princess, who was not without her day-dreams, like other young girls, had sometimes pictured to herself as coming on a splendid horse, with his followers around him in gallant attire, to ask her of her parents. He was well made and manly, with a bright and pleasant expression, and dressed, of course, to perfection. The Princess glanced at her plain black robe in vexation, and her fair face flushed.

'"I knew not,' she began. 'I thought I should see no one but the brown bull.'

"The Prince laughed merrily. He was in good spirits naturally, as any one would be who, after being forced for ten years to wear a frightful and hideous disguise, and to behave like a rough and surly bull, instead of like a well-born gentleman, should suddenly find himself in his own pleasant person again.

"'I *was* the bull,' he said, 'but you, Princess, have transformed me. How can I ever show you my gratitude?'

"'You owe me none,' said the Princess gently. 'What I did was to save my parents and their people. If it has served you in good stead, that for me is reward enough. But,' she added, 'I wish I had brought some of my pretty dresses with me. It must look so rude to you to have this ugly black one.'

"The Prince begged her not to trouble herself about such a trifle—to him she was beautiful as the day in whatever attire she happened to be. And then they ate their supper with a good appetite, though it seemed strange to the Princess to be quite without attendants, sitting alone at table with a young man whom she had never seen before.

"And after supper a new idea struck her.

"'Catch,' she said, drawing the first ball out of the little pocket in the front of her dress, where she always carried her balls, and flinging it across the table to the Prince with her usual skill, not breaking a glass or bending a leaf of the flowers with which the dishes were adorned.

"In an instant the Prince had caught it, and as she sent off the second, crying again 'Catch,' he returned her the first, leaving his hand free for the third.

"'Yes,' said the Princess, after continuing this game for a little while. 'Yes, I see that you are a true Prince,' for strange to say, he was as skilful at her game as she was herself.

"And they played with her balls for a long time throwing them higher and higher without ever missing, and laughing with pleasure, like two merry children.

"Then suddenly the Prince started from his seat, and his face grew sad and grave.

"'I must go,' he said; 'my hour of liberty is over.'

"'Go?" said the Princess in surprise and distress, for she had found the Prince a very pleasant companion. 'You must go? and leave me alone here?'

"'She looked as if she were going to cry, and the Prince looked as if he were going to cry too.

"'Alas, Princess!' he said, 'in my joy for the moment, I had almost forgotten my sad fate;' and then he went on to explain to her that for many years past he had been under a fairy spell, the work of an evil fairy who had vowed to revenge herself on his parents for some fancied insult to her. He had been forced to take the form of a bull and to spread terror wherever he went; and the power of this spell was to continue till he should meet with a beautiful Princess who of her own free will would return with him to his country and treat him with friendliness, both of which conditions had been now fulfilled.

"'Then all is right!' exclaimed the Princess joyfully. 'Why should you look so sad?'

"'Alas! no,' repeated the Prince, 'the spell is but partly broken. I have only power to regain my natural form for three hours every evening after sunset. And for three years more must it be so. Then, if your goodness continues so long, all will indeed be right. But during that time it will be necessary for you to live alone, except for the three hours I can pass with you, in this enchanted palace of mine. No harm will befall you, all your wants will be supplied by invisible hands; but for a young and beautiful Princess like you, it will be a sad trial, and one that I feel I have no right to ask your consent to.'

"'And can nothing be done?' said the Princess, 'nothing to shorten your endurance of the spell?'

"'Nothing,' said the Prince, sadly. 'Any effort to do so would only cause fearful troubles. I drop my hated skin at sunset, but three hours later I must resume it.'

"He glanced towards the corner of the room where, though the Princess had not before observed it, the brown bull's skin lay in a heap.

"'Hateful thing!' said the Princess, clenching her pretty hands, 'I would like to burn it.'

"The Prince grew pale with fright. 'Hush! Princess,' he said. 'Never breathe such words. Any rash act would have the most fearful consequences.'

"'What?' said the Princess, curiously.

"The Prince came nearer her and said in a low voice, 'For *me* they would be such. In such a case I might too probably never see you more.'

"The Princess blushed. Considering that he had spent ten years as a bull, it seemed to her that the Prince's manners were really not to be found fault with, and she promised him that she would consider the matter over, and by the next evening tell him her decision.

"She felt rather inclined to cry when she found herself again quite alone in the great strange palace, for she was only sixteen, even though so brave and cheerful. But still she had nothing whatever to complain of. Not a wish was formed in her heart but it was at once fulfilled, for this power was still the Prince's. She found, in what was evidently intended for her dressing-room, everything a young Princess could possibly desire in the shape of dresses, each more lovely than the others; shoes of silk or satin, exquisitely embroidered to suit her various costumes; laces and shawls, ribbons and feathers, and jewels of every conceivable kind in far greater abundance than so sensible a young lady found at all necessary. But believing all these pretty things to be provided to please her by the Prince's desire, she endeavoured to amuse herself with them, and found it rather interesting for the first time in her life to have to choose for herself. Her breakfasts and dinners, and everything conceivable in the shape of delicate and delicious food, appeared whenever she wished for anything of the kind; invisible hands opened the windows and shut the doors, lighted the lamps when the evening closed in, arranged her long fair hair more skilfully than any mortal maid, and brushed it softly when at night she wished to have it unfastened. Books in every language to interest her, for the Princess had been well taught, appeared on the tables, also materials for painting and for embroidery, in which she was very clever. Altogether it was impossible to complain, and the next day passed pleasantly enough, though it must be confessed the young Princess often found herself counting the hours till it should be that of sunset.

"Punctual to the moment the Prince made his appearance, but to his guest's distress he seemed careworn and anxious.

"'Has some new misfortune threatened you?' she asked.

"'No,' replied the Prince, 'but I have to-day scarcely been able to endure my anxiety to learn your decision. Never in all these terrible years has my suffering been greater, never have I so loathed the hideous disguise in which I am compelled to live.'

"Tears filled the Princess's eyes. Had anything been wanting to decide her, the deep pity which she now felt for the unfortunate Prince would have done so.

"'I *have* decided!' she exclaimed. 'Three years will soon pass, and I shall be well able to amuse myself with all the charming things with which I am surrounded. Besides, I shall see you every day, and the looking forward to that will help to cheer me.'

"It would be impossible to tell the Prince's delight. He became at once as gay and lively as the day before. The Princess and he had supper together, and amused themselves afterwards with the enchanted balls, and the evening passed so quickly that the Princess could hardly believe more than one hour instead of three had gone, when he started up, saying his time was over. It was sad to see him go, forced, through no fault of his own, to return to his hated disguise; but still it was with a lightened heart that the poor brown bull went tramping about during the next one-and-twenty hours.

"And on her side the Princess's lonely hours were cheered by the thought that she was to be the means of freeing him from the power of the terrible spell, for all that she saw of him only served to increase her sympathy and respect.

"So time went on. The Princess got more and more accustomed to her strange life, and every day more attached to the Prince, who on his side could not do enough to prove to her his gratitude. For many weeks he never failed to enter her presence the instant the sun had sunk below the horizon, and the three hours they spent together made amends to both for the loneliness of the rest of the day. And whenever the Princess felt inclined to murmur, she renewed her patience and courage by the thought of how much harder to bear was the Prince's share of the trial. She was allowed to remain in peaceful security, and to employ her time in pleasant and interesting ways; while he was forced to rove the world as a hateful monster, shunned by any of the human race whom he happened to meet, constantly exposed to fatigue and privation.

"Sometimes they spent a part of the evening in the beautiful gardens surrounding the palace. There, one day, as sunset was approaching, the Princess had betaken herself to wait the Prince's arrival, when a sad shock met her. It was past the usual hour of his coming. Several times she had wandered up and down the path by which he generally approached the castle, tossing her balls as she went, for more than once he had seen their glitter from a distance, and known by it that she was waiting. But this evening she waited and watched in vain, and at last, a strange anxiety seizing her, she turned towards the castle to see if possibly he had entered from the other side, and was hurrying back when a low moan reached her ears, causing her heart for an instant almost to leave off beating with terror.

CHAPTER X.

THE END OF THE BROWN BULL.

"'And happy they ever lived after'—
Yes, that was the end of the tale."

"THE Princess collected her courage, and turned in the direction of the sound. It seemed to come from a little thicket of close-growing bushes near which she had been passing. For a minute or two she could distinguish nothing, but another moan guided her in the right direction, and there, to her horror and distress, she saw the poor Prince lying on the ground, pale and death-like. At first she thought he was without consciousness, but when she hastened up to him with a cry, he opened his eyes.

"'Ah!' he said, faintly; 'I never thought I should have escaped alive. How good of you to have come to seek for me, Princess; otherwise I might have died here without seeing you again.'

"'But you must not die,' said the Princess, weeping; 'can nothing be done for you?'

"He tried to sit up, and when the Princess had fetched him some water from one of the numerous springs in the garden, he seemed better. But his right arm was badly injured.

"'How did it happen?' asked the Princess. 'I thought no mortal weapon had power to hurt you. That has been my only consolation through these lonely days of waiting.'

"'You are right,' replied the Prince; 'as a bull nothing can injure me, but in my own form I am in no way magically preserved. All day long I have been chased by hunters, who saw in me, I suppose, a valuable prize. I was terrified of the hour of sunset arriving and finding me far from home. I used my utmost endeavour to reach this in time, but, alas! I was overcome with fatigue, from which no spell protects me. At the entrance to these gardens I saw the sun disappear, and I fell exhausted, just as an arrow struck my right arm at the moment of my transformation. All I could do was to crawl in among these bushes, and here I have lain, thankful to escape from my persecutors, and most thankful to the happy thought, Princess, which brought you this way.'

"The Princess, her eyes still full of tears, helped him to the palace, where she bound up his arm and tended him carefully, for, young as she was, she had learnt many useful acts of this kind in her father's castle. The wound was not a very serious one; the Prince was suffering more from exhaustion and fatigue.

"'If I could spend a day or two here in peace,' he said sadly, 'I should quickly recover. But, alas! that is impossible. I must submit to my cruel fate. But this night I must confine my wanderings to the forests in this neighbourhood, where, perhaps, I may be able to hide from the huntsmen, who, no doubt, will be watching for me.'

"He sighed heavily, and the Princess's heart grew very sad.

"'I have little more than an hour left,' he said.

"'Yes,' said the Princess, 'sleep if you can; I will not disturb you.'

"And when she saw that he had fallen asleep she went into the other room, where in a corner lay the bull's skin, which the Prince had dragged behind him from the spot where it had fallen off as the sun sank.

"The Princess looked at it with a fierce expression, very different to the usual gentle look in her pretty eyes.

"'Hateful thing!' she said, giving it a kick with

her little foot; 'I wonder how I could get rid of you. Even if the Prince did risk never seeing me again, I am not sure but that it would be better for him than to lead this dreadful life.'

"And as her fancy pictured her poor Prince forced in this monstrous disguise to wander about all night tired and shelterless, her indignation rose beyond her control. She forgot where she was, she forgot the magic power that surrounded her, she forgot everything except her distress and anxiety.

"'Hateful thing!' she repeated, giving the skin another kick; 'I wish you were burnt to cinders.'

"Hardly had she said the words when a sudden noise like a clap of thunder shook the air; a flash of lightning seemed to glance past her and alight on the skin, which in an instant shrivelled up to a cinder like a burnt glove. Too startled at first to know whether she should rejoice or not, the Princess gazed at her work in bewilderment, when a voice of anguish, but, alas! a well-known voice, made her turn round. It was the Prince, hastening from the palace with an expression half of anger half of sorrowful reproach on his face.

"'O Princess, Princess,' he cried, 'what have you done? But a little more patience and all might have been well. And now I know not if I shall ever see you again.'

"'O Prince, forgive me, I did not mean it,' sobbed the poor Princess. 'I *will* see you again, and all shall yet be well.'

"'Seek for me across the hill of ice and the sea of glass,' said the Prince; but almost before the words had passed his lips a second thunderclap, louder and more terrific than the first, was heard. The Princess sank half fainting on the ground. When she again opened her eyes, Prince, palace, everything had disappeared. She was alone, quite alone, on a barren moorland, night coming on, and a cold cutting wind freezing the blood in her veins. And she was clothed in the plain black dress with which she had made her strange journey riding on the brown bull.

"It must be a dream, she thought, a terrible dream, and she shut her eyes again. But no, it was no dream, and soon her courage revived, and she began to ask herself what she should do.

"'Seek me beyond the hill of ice and the sea of glass,' the Prince had said; and she rose up to begin her weary journey. As she rose her hand came in contact with something hard in the folds of her dress; it was her golden balls. With the greatest delight she took them out of her pocket and looked at them. They were as bright and beautiful as ever, and the fairy's prophecy returned to the Princess's mind.

"'With my balls and my ready wit I shall yet conquer the evil powers that are against my poor Prince,' she said to herself cheerfully. 'Courage! all will be well."

"But there were sore trials to go through in the first place. The Princess set off on her journey. She had to walk many weary miles across the moor, the cold wind blowing in her face, the rough ground pricking her tender feet. But she walked on and on till at last the morning broke and she saw a road before her, bordered on one side by a forest of trees, for she had reached the extreme edge of the moor. She had gone but a little way when she came to a small and miserable hovel, from which issued feeble sounds of distress. The Princess went up to the door and looked in—a very old woman sat huddled up in a corner weeping and lamenting herself.

"'What is the matter, my friend?' asked the Princess.

"'Matter enough,' replied the old woman. 'I cannot light my fire, and I am bitterly cold. Either the sticks are wet, or the strength has gone out of my poor old arms.'

"'Let me help you,' said the Princess. 'My arms are strong enough.'

"She took the sticks and arranged them cleverly in the fireplace, and just as she was choosing two of the driest to rub together to get a light, one of her balls dropped out of her pocket. It fell on to the piled-up wood, and immediately a bright flame danced up the chimney. The Princess picked up her ball and put it back in her pocket, cheered and encouraged by this proof of their magic power. The old woman came near to the fire, and stretched out her withered hands to the blaze.

"'What can I do for you, my pretty lady,' she said, 'in return for your good nature?'

"'Give me a cup of milk to refresh me for my journey,' said the Princess. 'And perhaps, too, you can tell me something about my journey. Are the hill of ice and the sea of glass anywhere in this neighbourhood?'

"The old woman smiled and nodded her head two or three times.

"'Seven days must you travel,' she said, 'before you see them. At the foot of the hill of ice lies the sea of glass. No mortal foot unaided has ever crossed the one or ascended the other. Here, take these shoes—with them you can safely walk over the sea of glass, and with this staff you can mount the hill of ice,' and as she spoke she handed to the Princess a pair of curiously carved wooden shoes and a short sharp-pointed stick. The Princess took them gratefully, and would have thanked the old woman, whom she now knew to be a fairy, but she stopped her. "'Think not,' she said, 'that your difficulties will be over when you have reached the summit of the hill of ice. But all I can do for you more is to give you this nut, which you must open in your moment of sorest perplexity.'

"And as the Princess held out her hand for the nut the old woman had disappeared.

"But refreshed and encouraged the Princess left the cottage, carrying with her her three gifts, and prepared to face all the perils of her journey with an undaunted heart.

"It would be impossible to describe all she went through during the seven days which passed before she reached the sea of glass. She saw some strange and wonderful sights, for in those days the world was very different from what it is now. She was often tired and hungry, thankful for a cup of milk or crust of bread from those she happened to meet on the way.

But her courage never failed her, and at last, on the morning of the eighth day, she saw shining before her in the sunlight the great silent sea of glass of which she had been told.

"It would have been hopeless to attempt to cross it without fairy aid, for it was polished more brightly than any mirror, and so hard that no young Princess's bones could have borne a fall on its cruel surface. But with the magic shoes there was less than no difficulty, for no sooner had the Princess slipped her feet into them than they turned into skates, and very wonderful skates, for they possessed the power of enabling their wearer to glide along with the greatest swiftness. The Princess had never skated in her life, and she was delighted.

"'Next to flying,' she said to herself, 'nothing could be pleasanter,' and she was almost sorry when her skim across the sea of glass was over, and she found herself at the foot of the hill of ice.

"She looked upwards with something like despair. It was a terrible ascent to attempt, for the mountain was all but straight, so steep were its sides of hard, clear, sparkling ice. The Princess looked at her feet, the magic shoes had already disappeared; she looked at the staff she still held in her hand—how could a stick help her up such a mountain? and half impatiently, half hopelessly, she threw it from her. Instantly it stretched itself out, growing wider and wider, the notches in the wood expanding, till it had taken the shape of a roughly-made ladder of irregular steps, hooked on to the ice by the sharp spike at its end, and the Princess, ashamed of her discouragement, mounted up the steps without difficulty, and as she reached the top one, of itself the ladder pushed up before her, so that she could mount straight up without hesitation.

"She stepped forward bravely. It took a long time, even though she had the fairy aid, and by the time she reached the top of the hill night had fallen, and but for the light of the stars, she would not have known where to step. A long plain stretched before her—no trees or bushes even broke the wide expanse. There was no shelter of any kind, and the Princess found herself obliged to walk on and on, for the wind was very cold, and she dared not let herself rest. This night and the next day were the hardest part of all the journey, and seemed even more so, because the Princess had hoped that the sea of glass and the hill of ice were to be the worst of her difficulties. More than once she was tempted to crack the nut, the last of the old woman's presents, but she refrained, saying to herself she might yet be in greater need, and she walked on and on, though nearly dead with cold and fatigue, till late in the afternoon. Then at last, far before her still, she saw gleaming the lights of a city, and, encouraged by the sight, she gathered her courage together and pressed on, till, at the door of a little cottage at the outskirts of the town, she sank down with fatigue. An old woman, with a kind face, came out of the house and invited her to enter and rest.

"'You look sorely tired, my child,' she said. 'Have you travelled far?'

"'Ah yes!' replied the poor Princess, 'very far. I am nearly dead with fatigue;' and indeed she looked very miserable. Her beautiful fair hair was all tumbled and soiled, her poor little feet were scratched and blistered, her black dress torn and draggled—she looked far more like a beggar-maiden than like a princess. But yet, her pretty way of speaking and gentle manners showed she was not what she seemed, and when she had washed her face and combed her hair, the old woman looked at her with admiration.

"''Tis a pity you have not a better dress,' she said, 'for then you could have gone with me to see the rejoicings in the town for the marriage of our Prince.'

"'Is your Prince to be married to-day?' asked the Princess.

"'No, not to-day—to-morrow,' said the old woman. 'But the strange thing is that it is not yet known who is to be his bride. The Prince has only lately returned to his home, for, for many years, he has been shut up by a fairy spell in a beautiful palace in the north, and now that the spell is broken and he is restored to his parents, they are anxious to see him married. But he must still be under a spell of some kind, they say, for though he has all that heart can wish, he is ever sad and silent, and as if he were thinking of something far away. And he has said that he will marry no princess but one who can catch three golden balls at a time, as if young princesses were brought up to be jugglers! Nevertheless, all the princesses far and wide have been practising their best at catching balls, and to-morrow the great feasts are to begin, and she who catches best is to be chosen out of all the princesses as the bride of our Prince.'

"The poor Princess listened with a beating heart to the old woman's talk. There could be no doubt as to who the Prince of this country was.

"'I have come but just in time,' she said to herself, and then she rose, and thanking her hostess for her kindness, said she must be going.

"'But where are you going, you poor child?' said the old woman. 'You look far too tired to go farther, and for two or three days all these rejoicings will make the country unpleasant for a young girl to travel through alone. Stay with me till you are rested.'

"The Princess thanked her with tears in her eyes for her kindness. 'I have nothing to reward you with,' she said, 'but some day I may be able to do so,' and then she thankfully accepted her offer.

"'And to-morrow,' said the old woman, 'you must smarten yourself up as well as you can, and then we shall go out to see the gay doings.'

"But the Princess lay awake all night thinking what she should do to make herself known to her faithful Prince.

"The next day the old woman went out early to hear all about the festivities. She came back greatly excited.

"'Come quickly,' she said. "The crowd is so great that no one will notice your poor clothes. And, indeed, among all the pretty girls there will be none prettier than you," she added, looking admiringly at the Princess, who had arranged her beautiful hair and brushed her soiled dress, and who looked sweeter than ever now that she was rested and refreshed. 'There are three princesses who have come to the feast,' she went on, 'the first from the south, the second from the east, the third from the west, each more beautiful than another, the people say. The trial of the golden balls is to be in the great hall of the palace, and a friend of mine has promised me a place at one of the windows which overlook it, so that we can see the whole;' and the Princess, feeling as if she were in a dream, rose up to accompany the old woman, her balls and her precious nut in her pocket.

"They made their way through the crowd and placed themselves at the window, as the old woman had said. The Princess looked down at the great hall below, all magnificently decorated and already filled with spectators. Suddenly the trumpet sounded, and the Prince in whose honour was all the rejoicing entered. At sight of him—her own Prince indeed, but looking so strangely pale and sad that she would hardly have recognised him—the Princess could not restrain a little cry.

"'What is it?' said the old woman.

"'A passer-by trod on my foot,' said the Princess, fearful of attracting attention. And the old woman said no more, for at this moment another blast of trumpets announced the arrival of the princesses, who were to make the trial of the balls. The first was tall and dark, with raven tresses and brilliant, flashing eyes. She was dressed in a robe of rich maize colour, and as she took her place on the dais she looked round her, as if to say, 'Who can compete with me in beauty or in skill?' And she was the Princess of the south.

"The second was also tall, and her hair was of a deep rich brown, and her eyes were sparkling and her cheeks rosy. She was dressed in bright pink, and laughed as she came forward, as if sure of herself and her attractions. And she was the Princess of the east.

"The third moved slowly, and as if she cared little what was thought of her, so confident was she of her pre-eminence. She wore a blue robe, and her face was pale and her eyes cold, though beautiful. And her hair had a reddish tinge, but yet she too was beautiful. And she was the Princess of the west.

"The Prince bowed low to each, but no smile lit up his grave face, and his glance rested but an instant on each fair Princess as she approached.

"'Are these ladies all?' he asked, in a low voice, as if expecting yet more. And when the answer came, 'Yes, these are all,' a still deeper melancholy settled on his face, and he seemed indifferent to all about him.

"Then the trial began. The Prince had three golden balls, one of which he offered to each Princess. They took them, and each threw one back to him. Then one after another, as quick as lightning, he threw all three to the yellow Princess. She caught them all and threw them back; again he returned them, but the first only, reached her hand, the second and third fell to the ground, and with another low bow the Prince turned from her, and her proud face grew scarlet with anger. The pink Princess fared no better. She was laughing so, as if to show her confidence, that she missed the third ball, even at the first throw, and when the Prince turned also from her she laughed again, though this time her laughter was not all mirth. Then the cold blue Princess came forward. She caught the balls better, but at the third throw, one of them rising higher than the others, she would not trouble herself to stretch her arm out farther, so it fell to the ground, and as the Prince turned from her likewise, a great silence came over the crowd.

"Suddenly a cry arose. 'A fourth Princess,' the

people shouted, and the old woman up at the window was so eager to see the new-comer that she did not notice that her companion had disappeared. She had watched the failure of the two first Princesses, then seeing what was coming she had quietly made her way through the crowd to a hidden corner behind the great pillars of the hall. There, her hands trembling with eagerness, she drew forth from the magic nut, which she had cracked with her pretty teeth, a wonderful fairy robe of spotless white. In an instant her black dress was thrown to her feet, and the white garment, which fitted her as if by magic, had taken its place. Never was Princess dressed in such a hurry, but never was toilette more successful. And as the cry arose of 'A fourth Princess' she made her way up the hall. From one end to the other she came, rapidly making her way through the crowd, which cleared before her in surprise and admiration, for as she walked she threw before her, catching them ever as she went, her golden balls. Her fair hair floated on her shoulders, her white robe gleamed like snow, her sweet face, flushed with hope and eagerness, was like that of a happy child, her eyes saw nothing but the one figure standing at the far end of the hall, the figure of the Prince, who, as the cry reached his ears, started forward with a hope he hardly dared encourage, holding out his hands as she came nearer and yet nearer in joyfulness of welcome.

"But she waved him back—then, taking her place where the other Princesses had stood, she threw her balls, one, two, three; in an instant they were caught by the Prince, and returned to her like flashes of lightning over and over again, never failing, never falling, as if attached by invisible cords, till at last a great cry arose from the crowds, and the Prince led forward, full in the view of the people, his beautiful bride, his true Princess.

"Then all her troubles were forgotten, and every one rejoiced, save perhaps the three unsuccessful Princesses, who consoled themselves by saying there was magic in it, and so possibly there was. But there is more than one kind of magic, and some kinds, it is to be hoped, the world will never be without. And messengers were sent to summon to the wedding the father and mother of the Princess, who all this time had been in doubt and anxiety as to the fate of their dear child. And the kind old woman who had sheltered her in her poverty and distress was not forgotten."

The voice stopped—for a minute or two the

children sat silent, not sure if they were to hear anything else. Strangely enough, as the story went on, it seemed more and more as if it were Marcelline's voice that was telling it, and at last Hugh looked up to see if it was still the white lady, whose knee his head was resting on. Jeanne too looked up at the same moment, and both children gave a little cry of surprise. The white lady had disappeared, and it was indeed Marcelline who was in her place. The white room, the white chairs, the white cats, the spinning-wheel, and the pointed windows, had all gone, and instead there was old Marcelline with her knitting-needles gently clicking in a regular way, that somehow to Hugh seemed mixed up with his remembrance of the soft whirr of the wheel, her neatly frilled cap round her face, and her bright dark eyes smiling down at the children. Hugh felt so sorry and disappointed that he shut his eyes tight and tried to go on dreaming, if indeed dreaming it was. But it was no use. He leant his face against Marcelline's soft white apron and tried to fancy it the fairy lady's fairy robe; but it was no use. He had to sit up and look about him.

"Well," said Marcelline, "and didn't you like the story?"

Hugh looked at Jeanne. It couldn't be a dream then—there *had* been a story, for if he had been asleep, of course he couldn't have heard it. He said nothing, however—he waited to see what Jeanne would say. Jeanne tossed back her head impatiently.

"Of course I liked it," she said. "It's a beautiful story. But, Marcelline, how did you turn into yourself—*was* it you all the time? Why didn't you leave us with the white lady?"

Hugh was so pleased at what Jeanne said that he didn't mind a bit about Marcelline having taken the place of the white lady. Jeanne was the same as he was—that was all he cared about. He jumped up eagerly—they were in Jeanne's room, close to the fire, and both Jeanne and he had their little red flannel dressing-gowns on.

"How did these come here?" he said, touching the sleeve of his own one.

"Yes," said Jeanne. "And where are our wings, if you please, Mrs. Marcelline?"

Marcelline only smiled.

"I went to fetch you," she said, "and of course I didn't want you to catch cold on the way back."

But that was *all* they could get her to say, and then she carried them off to bed, and they both slept soundly till morning.

CHAPTER XI.

DUDU'S OLD STORY.

"It was not a story, however,
But just of old days that had been."

CHILD NATURE.

It was queer, but so it was. The children said very little to each other the next day of their new adventures. Only Hugh felt satisfied that this time little Jeanne had forgotten nothing; daylight Jeanne and moonlight Jeanne were the same. Yet he had a feeling that if he said much about it, if he persisted in trying to convince Jeanne that he had been right all through, he might spoil it all. It would be like seizing the fairy lady's cobweb threads roughly, and spoiling them, and finding you had nothing left. He felt now quite content to let it all be like a pretty dream which they both knew about, but which was not for everyday life.

Only one impression remained on his mind. He got the greatest wish to learn to throw balls like the princess of the Brown Bull story, and for some days every time they went out, he kept peering in at the toy-shop windows to see if such a thing as golden balls was to be had. And at last Jeanne asked him what he was always looking for, and then he told her.

She agreed with him that golden balls would be a very pretty play, but she was afraid such a thing could not be found.

"They were fairy balls, you know, Chéri," she said, gravely.

"Yes," Hugh replied, "he knew they were; he did not expect such balls as they were, of course, but still he didn't see why they might not get some sort of gold-looking balls. There were red and blue, and green ones in plenty. He didn't see why there should be no gold ones."

"Gold is so very dear," said Jeanne.

"Yes, real gold is, of course," said Hugh; "but there are lots of things that look like gold that can't be real gold—picture frames, and the edges of books, and lots of other things."

"Yes," said Jeanne, "but still, I don't see that the

stuff any of those are made of would do to make balls of."

However, she joined Hugh in the search, and many a day when they were out they peeped together not only into the toy-shops, but into the windows of the queer old curiosity shops, of which, in the ancient town which was Jeanne's home, there were many. And at last one day they told Marcelline what it was they were so anxious to find. She shook her head. There was no such toy in *this* country, she said, but she did not laugh at them, or seem to think them silly. And she advised them to be content with the prettiest balls they *could* get, which were of nice smooth buff-coloured leather, very well made, and neither too soft nor too hard. And in the sunlight, said Jeanne, they really had rather a shiny, goldy look.

For several days to come these balls were a great interest to the children. Early and late they were practising at them, and, with patience and perseverance, they before long arrived at a good deal of skill. Jeanne was the quicker in the first place, but Hugh was so patient that he soon equalled her, and then the interest grew still greater.

"I really think, Chéri," said Jeanne, one evening,

when they had been playing for a good while, "I really think our balls are *getting* to be rather like fairy ones. Every day they go better and better."

"Perhaps it is our hands that are getting to be like fairy ones," said Hugh. "But it is growing too dark to see to play any more."

They were playing in the tapestry room, for Marcelline had told them they would have more space there, as it was large, and Hugh's little bed in the corner did not take up much room. It was getting dusk, for the days were not yet very long, though winter was almost over, and they had been playing a good while. As Hugh spoke he gave the last ball a final throw high up in the air, higher than usual, for though Jeanne sprang forward to catch it, she missed it somehow. It dropped to the ground behind her.

"O Chéri!" she cried, reproachfully, "that is the first time I have missed. Oh dear, where can the ball have gone to?"

She stooped down to look for it, and in a minute Hugh was down beside her. They felt all about, creeping on their hands and knees, but the missing ball was not to be so easily found.

"It must have got behind the tapestry," said Hugh, pulling back as he spoke, a corner of the hang-ings close to where he and Jeanne were, which seemed loose. And at the same moment both children gave a little cry of astonishment. Instead of the bare wall which they expected to see, or to feel rather, behind the tapestry, a flight of steps met their view—a rather narrow flight of steps running straight upwards, without twisting or turning, and lighted from above by a curious hanging lamp, hanging by long chains from a roof high up, which they could not see.

"Why, is this a new part of the house?" cried Hugh. "Jeanne, did you know there were stairs behind the tapestry?"

"No, of course not," said Jeanne. "It must be a part of our house, I suppose, but I never saw it before. Shall we go up, Chéri, and see where it takes us to? Perhaps it's another way to the white lady's turret, and she'll tell us another story."

"No," said Hugh, "I don't believe it leads to her turret, and I don't think we could find our way there again. She seemed to mean we could never go again, I think. But we may as well go up this stair, and see what we do find, Jeanne."

And just at that moment a funny thing happened. They heard a little noise, and looking up, there—hopping down the stair before them, step by step, as if some one had started it from the top, came the lost ball, or what the children thought the lost ball, for with an exclamation Hugh darted forward to pick it up, and held it out to Jeanne. But Jeanne looked at it with astonishment.

"Why, Chéri," she cried, "it's turned into gold."

So it was, or at least into something which looked just like it.

"Chéri," Jeanne went on, her eyes dancing with excitement, "I do believe this is another way into Fairyland, or into some other queer place like what we've seen. Come on, quick."

The children seized hold of each other's hands, and hurried up the stair. The steps were easier to mount than those of the corkscrew staircase up to the white lady's turret, and very soon the children found themselves at the top of the first flight. There, looking upwards, they could see the roof. It was a sort of cupola; the chains from which the lamps hung were fastened to the centre, but the rest of the roof was of glass, and through it the children saw the sky, already quite dark, and with innumerable stars dotting its surface.

"Come on, Chéri," said Jeanne; "I believe this stair leads out on to the roof of the house."

So it did. A door at the top opened as they ran up the last steps, and a familiar figure stepped out.

"Dudu!" exclaimed Jeanne, in a tone of some disappointment.

"Did you not expect to see me?" said the raven. "Why, I thought it would amuse you to come up here and see the stars."

"So it will," said Hugh, anxious to make up for Jeanne's abruptness. "But, you see, we thought—at least we hoped—we should find some new adventures up here, especially when the ball hopped down the stairs, all gold."

"What did you expect?" said Dudu, cocking his head. "Fairies, I suppose, or enchanted princesses, or something of that kind. What creatures children are for wonders, to be sure."

"Now, Dudu," said Jeanne, "you needn't talk that way. Whether we're fond of wonders or not, anyhow it's you that's given us them to be fond of. It was you that sent us to the frogs' country, and all that, and it was you that took us to hear the white lady's story. So you're not to laugh at us, and you must find us some more adventures, now you've brought us up here."

"Adventures don't grow on every tree, Mademoiselle Jeanne," remarked Dudu.

"Well, *Dudus* don't either," replied Jeanne; "but as we've got *you*, you see, it all depends on you to get us the adventures. I know you can, if you like."

Dudu shook his head.

"No," he said, "there are many things I can't do. But come out on to the roof, we can talk there just as well."

He just turned towards the door by which he had entered, and it opened of itself. He hopped through, and the children followed him. They found themselves, as Dudu had said, on the roof of the house, of a part of the house, that is to say. It seemed more like the roof of a little tower or turret.

Hugh and Jeanne stood for a moment or two in silence, looking up at the brilliant show of stars overhead. It was not cold, the air seemed peculiarly fresh and sweet, as if it were purer and finer than that lower down.

"It's rather nice up here, eh?" said Dudu.

"Yes, very," replied Hugh. "We're very much obliged to you for bringing us up here. Aren't we, Jeanne?"

"Yes," said Jeanne, "not counting fairies and adventures that's to say, it's very nice up here."

"I often come up here at night," said Dudu. "I wonder how many thousand times I've been up here."

"Are you so very old, Dudu?" said Jeanne, "as old as the white lady?"

"I daresay," said Dudu, vaguely—he seemed to be thinking to himself. "Yes," he continued, cocking his head on one side, "I suppose I am what *you* would call very old, though the white lady would consider me quite a baby. Yes, I've seen queer things in my time."

"*What?*" said the children both together, eagerly, "oh, do tell us some of them. If you would tell us a story, Dudu, it would be as nice as an adventure."

"Stories," said Dudu, "are hardly in my line. I might tell you a little of some things I've seen, but I don't know that they would interest you."

"Oh yes! oh yes!" cried the children, "of course they would. And it's so nice and warm up here, Dudu—much warmer than in the house."

"Sit down, then," said Dudu, "here, in this corner. You can lean against the parapet,"—for a low wall ran round the roof—"and look at the stars while you listen to me. Well—one day, a good long while ago you would consider it, no doubt——"

"Was it a hundred years ago?" interrupted Jeanne.

"About that, I daresay," said the raven carelessly. "I cannot be quite exact to twenty or thirty years, or so. Well, one day—it was a very hot day, I remember, and I had come up here for a little change of air—I was standing on the edge of the parapet watching our two young ladies who were walking up and down the terrace path down there, and thinking how nice they looked in their white dresses and blue sashes tied close up under their arms, like the picture of your great-grandmother as a young girl, in the great salon, Mademoiselle Jeanne."

"Oh yes, I know it," said Jeanne. "She has a nice face, but *I* don't think her dress is at all pretty, Dudu."

"And I don't suppose your great-grandmother would think yours at all pretty, either, Mademoiselle Jeanne," said Dudu, with the queer sort of croak which he used for a laugh. "It is one of the things that has amazed me very much in my observations—the strange fancies the human race has about clothes. Of course you are not so fortunate as we are in having them ready-made, but still I cannot understand why you don't do the best you can—adopt a pattern and keep to it always. It would be the next best thing to having feathers, *I* should say."

"I don't think so," said Jeanne. "It would be very stupid every morning when you got up, and every time you were going out, or friends coming to see you, or anything like that—it would be *very* stupid never to have to think, 'What shall I put on?' or to plan what colours would look nice together. There would hardly be any use in having shops or dressmakers, or anything. And *certainly*, Monsieur Dudu, I wouldn't choose to be dressed like you, never anything but black—as if one were always going to a funeral."

"It is all a matter of taste, Mademoiselle," replied Dudu, so amiably that Hugh wondered more and more at his politeness to Jeanne, who was certainly not very civil to him. "For my part, I confess I have always had a great fancy for white—the force of contrast, I suppose—and this brings me back to telling you how very nice your great-grandmother and her sister looked that day walking up and down the terrace path in their white dresses."

"My great-grandmother!" exclaimed Jeanne. "Why, you said 'our young ladies.'"

"So they were our young ladies," replied Dudu. "Even though one was your great-grandmother, Mademoiselle, and not yours only but Monsieur Chéri's too, and the other, of course, your great-grand-aunt. There have been many 'our young ladies' that I can remember in this house, which has so long been the home of one family, and my home always. In three or four hundred years one sees a good deal. Ah yes! Well, as I was saying, I was standing on the edge of the parapet looking over at the young ladies, and admiring them and the sunshine and the flowers in the garden all at once, when I suddenly heard a window open. It was not one of the windows of our house. I have very quick ears, and I knew that in an instant, so I looked about to see what window it was. In those days there were not quite so many houses behind our garden as there are now. Your great-great-grandfather sold some of the land about that time, and then houses were built, but just then there were only two or three that overlooked one side of the garden. One of them was a large high house, which was let in flats to various families, often visitors to the town, or strangers who had come for a short time for the education of their children, or some other reason. It was not long before I discovered that the window I had heard open was in this house. It was one on the second story, looking on to a little balcony which at one end was not very high above the terrace walk. I watched to see who had opened the window, and in a few moments I saw peeping out half timidly the pretty fair face of a little girl. Quite a little girl she was, not much older than you, Mademoiselle Jeanne, but not like you, for she had light hair and soft blue eyes, and a fair face like Monsieur Chéri. She was a little English girl. She peeped out, and then, seeing that no one was observing her, she came quietly on to the balcony, and, creeping down into a corner where she could scarcely be seen, she sat watching our two pretty young ladies with all her eyes. No wonder, I thought; they were very pretty young ladies, and it was nice to see them together, walking up and down with arms intertwined, and talking eagerly, their talk sometimes interrupted by merry bursts of soft girlish laughter. And all the time the lonely little creature on the balcony sat and watched them longingly, her little pale face pressed against the bars, her plain black dress almost hiding her from notice.

"'How happy they look, those pretty young ladies,' the lonely little girl said to herself. 'How happy I should be if I had a sister, for I have no one to talk to, no one to kiss me and play with me and if ever I say I am sad my aunt is angry. O mother! why did you go away and leave me?'"

"Could you hear all that from up here on the roof?" said Jeanne. "Dear me, Dudu, you must have good ears."

"Of course I have; I told you so, Mademoiselle," said Dudu drily. "I had better ears than your great-grandmother and her sister, for they heard nothing, not even when the poor little girl took courage to push her face farther forward between the railings, and to say very softly and timidly,

"'Mesdemoiselles, Mesdemoiselles, *might* I come and walk with you? I am so tired of being here all alone.'

"They did not hear her. They were talking too busily about the fête of their mother, I think, which was to be in a few days, and of what they were to prepare for her. And the poor little girl sat up there for more than an hour watching them with longing eyes, but not daring to call out more loudly. It made me quite melancholy to see her, and when at last our young ladies went in, and she had to give up hopes of gaining their attention, it made me more melancholy still, she looked so disappointed, and her eyes were full of tears ; and I felt quite upset about her, and kept turning over in my head what I could do to make her happier. I thought about it for some time, and at last I decided that the first thing to do was to find out more about the little stranger and the cause of her grief. For this purpose I stationed myself the next morning just below the window of the kitchen of her house, which, by hopping from the balcony, I was easily able to do, and by listening to the conversation of the servants I soon learned all I wanted to know. She was, as I had supposed, a little English girl. Her mother had died in Italy but a short time before, and she was now in the charge of her mother's aunt, an elderly and severe lady, who understood nothing about children, and took no pains to make poor little Charlotte happy. So it was a sad life for the child, whose father also was dead ; and as from the talk of the servants I gathered that she was a good and gentle little girl, I felt more sorry for her than before ; and as I hopped back on to the balcony I looked to see if she was again at the window. Yes, there she was, her face pressed against the glass, staring out in the direction of the terrace walk, watching, no doubt, to see if our young ladies were coming out again. I hopped in front of the window backwards and forwards two or three times to catch her attention, and a smile lit up her little pale face when she saw me.

"'Good day, Mr. Raven,' she said politely. 'Have you come to see me? It is very kind of you if you have, for I have nobody to play with. But, oh! if you could tell those pretty young ladies how I should like to walk about their garden with them, how pleased I should be.'

"I bowed to her in token of understanding what she said, but I was not sure that she noticed it, for she just went on chattering in her soft little voice.

"'Poor old raven,' she said. 'What a pity you can't speak, for if you could I might send a message by you to those pretty young ladies;' and though I walked slowly backwards and forwards on the balcony, and bowed most politely each time I passed her, yet she did not seem to understand."

"Why didn't you speak?" interrupted Jeanne. "You can speak quite well to Chéri and me. Had you not learned to speak at that time, Dudu?"

The raven hemmed and hawed and cleared his throat.

"It is not to the point, Mademoiselle," he said,

"to enter into all these explanations. If you would have the goodness to let me continue my reminiscences without interrupting me, I should really be obliged. I warned you I had not any amusing stories to tell, merely recollections of scenes in my past life. If you would prefer my leaving off, you have only to say so."

"Oh no, no. Please go on," exclaimed Jeanne, seeing that the raven was really ruffled. "I think it's *very* interesting, and I'll promise not to interrupt you any more."

"Well," continued Dudu, "I bowed, as I told you, very politely two or three times, and at last I hopped away, still revolving in my mind how I could serve the poor little girl. That afternoon our young ladies came again on to the terrace, but they did not stay long, and the little girl was not to be seen on the balcony, though I daresay she was peering out through the window to see as far as she could. And the next day and the day after were very rainy, so there was nothing I could do. But after that again there came a very fine day—a beautiful sunny day it was, I remember it well—and our young ladies came out like the flowers and the birds to enjoy it. Out, too, came the forlorn little black figure, hiding itself as before behind the railings of the balcony, but looking with longing eyes at the garden below, which to her must have seemed a kind of Paradise. I directed my steps to the terrace, and walked slowly in front of the young ladies, slowly and solemnly straight in front of them, for I wanted to attract their attention.

"'How particularly solemn Dudu looks to-day,' said one of them to the other.

"'Yes,' she replied, 'quite as if he had something on his mind. Have you been doing anything naughty, Dudu?'

"I turned and looked at her reproachfully. I was not offended, I knew she was only joking, my character stood far above any imputation; but still, there are subjects on which jokes are better avoided, and there *was* a cousin of mine whose honesty, I am sorry to say, had been more than once suspected; altogether, I hardly thought the remark in good taste, and Mademoiselle Eliane was not slow to perceive it.

"'Poor old Dudu,' she cried; 'have I hurt your feelings? But tell me what are you looking so solemn about?'

"I looked at her again, and then, sure that she

and her sister were both watching me with attention, I sprang up the side of the wall next the little stranger's house, hopped over the balcony railings, and finding, as I expected, my little friend crouched down in the corner, I gave a loud, sharp croak, as if something were the matter. Charlotte started up in a fright, and the young ladies, watching me curiously, for the first time observed her little figure.

"'Why, Dudu has a friend up there!' exclaimed Mademoiselle Jeanne—your great-grandmother, my dears. 'Mademoiselle,' she called out to the little girl, whose small black figure did not look very much bigger than mine as we stood up there side by side; 'Mademoiselle, do not be frightened of our old raven. He will not hurt you.'

"'I am not frightened, thank you,' said the little girl's gentle voice. 'He has been to see me before. I was only startled when he made that funny noise. But O Mesdemoiselles,' she continued, clasping her hands in entreaty, 'you do not know how I should like to come down into your garden and play with you, or at least,' as she suddenly recollected that such tall young ladies were rather past the age for mere 'playing,' 'walk about and talk with you. I have watched you so many days, and I am so lonely.

But I did not like to speak to you unless you spoke to me.'

"'We never saw you,' said Mademoiselle Eliane. 'We should not have seen you now but for the funny way Dudu has been going on, as if he wanted to introduce us to each other.'

"I felt quite proud when Mademoiselle Eliane said that. It has always been a gratification to me to find myself understood. And I felt still prouder when the little girl replied, looking at me gratefully,

"'How nice of him! He must have understood what I said to him in fun the other day. But O Mesdemoiselles,' she went on, '*may* I come down to you?'

"'How can you get down?' said Mademoiselle Jeanne; 'and are you sure your mother would not mind?'

"'I have no mother,' said the little girl sadly, 'and my aunt would not mind, I know. She never minds what I do, if I don't make a noise.'

"'But how can you get down?' repeated Mademoiselle Jeanne, 'unless Dudu can take you on his back and fly down with you!'

"'Oh, I can easily get down,' said the little girl; 'I have often planned it. I can climb over the railings at this end—look, there is a jutting-out ledge that I can put my foot on. Then I can stand a minute outside and jump—if you will come close to, so that I shall not roll down the terrace bank.'

CHAPTER XII.

AU REVOIR.

> "One after another they flew away
> Far up to the heavenly blue,
> To the better country, the upper day——"
>
> JEAN INGELOW.

"LITTLE Charlotte climbed over the railings," continued Dudu, "but she did not jump down on the other side, for Mademoiselle Eliane, who was tall, found that by standing half-way up the bank she could reach the child and hand her down to Mademoiselle Jeanne, a little way below. There was a good deal of laughing over it all, and this helped them to make friends more quickly than anything else would have done. But indeed Charlotte was not a shy child, she had travelled too much and seen too many people to be so, and our young ladies, besides, were so kind and merry that no little girl could long have been strange with them. She ran about the garden in the greatest delight; her new friends showed her all their favourite nooks, and allowed her to make a bouquet of the flowers she liked best; and when they were tired of standing about they all sat down together on a bank, and Charlotte told to the young ladies the story of her short life. It was a sad little story; her father had died when she was very young, and her mother, whose health had never been good after the shock of his death, had gone to Italy with the aunt who had brought her up, in hopes of growing stronger. But through two or three years of sometimes seeming better and sometimes worse, she had really been steadily failing, and at last she died, leaving her poor little girl almost alone, 'for the old aunt was now,' said Charlotte, 'always ill, and not ill as mamma used to be,' she added, for however tired *she* was, she always liked her little girl to be beside her, and never wearied of listening to all she had to say.

"'But now,' said the child, 'I am always alone, and it is *so* sad. And I have watched you so often from the balcony, and wished I might come down to you. And now, if you will let me come to see you every day, I shall be *so* happy.'

"She was a dear little girl, so sweet, and simple,

and loving. She quite gained our young ladies' hearts with her pretty ways and her funny little English accent. They kissed her on both cheeks, and told her they would be very pleased for her to come to them in the garden whenever she saw them from the balcony, as she was so sure her aunt would not object to it. They could not invite her to the house, they explained, unless their mother and her aunt had made acquaintance. Of course it would not have done, as little Charlotte quite understood; for in those days," Dudu observed in passing, "politeness and ceremony were much more observed than is at present, I am sorry to say, the case.

"The little English girl, however," he went on, "was only too delighted to have received permission to visit them in their garden. And not many days passed on which she did not join them there. It was a lovely summer that year—I remember it so well. Never now does the sun seem to me to shine quite so brightly as in those days. Perhaps it is that I am growing old, perhaps the sad days that soon after followed left a cloud on my memory and a mist on my spirit which have never since entirely cleared away; however that may be, I never remember so bright and beautiful a summer as the one I am telling you of. And little Charlotte's merry laugh was often heard on the terrace walk, as she ran races with Mademoiselle Eliane's dog, or made daisy wreaths for Mademoiselle Jeanne's dark hair. Kindness and companionship were all she required to make her a bright and happy child. But the pleasant summer faded, and with the first autumn days came a fresh sorrow for the little girl. One morning, before the usual time for meeting in the garden, I caught sight of her on the balcony, her face looking again like the little pale Charlotte I had first known her, her eyes red with weeping. And as by good chance the young ladies came out soon the reason was soon explained.

"'I am going away, my dear young ladies,' cried Charlotte, as she threw herself into their arms. 'My aunt has just told me. We return to England in a few days. To England, where I have no friends, where I shall be again all alone. O Mademoiselle Eliane! O Mademoiselle Jeanne! what shall I do without you, and your pretty garden, and your kindness, and poor old Dudu, and the flowers, and everything?'

"They consoled her as well as they could, my kind young ladies, whose hearts were always full of sympathy. But the tears came to their own eyes when they saw how real and acute was the little girl's grief.

"'You will come back to see us again, little Charlotte, perhaps,' they said. 'Your aunt has travelled so much, very likely she will not wish to remain always in England. And you would always find us here—in the winter at any rate; generally in the summer we spend some months at our château, though this summer our father had business which obliged him to stay here. But for that we should not have seen you so much.'

"But Charlotte was not to be consoled. Her aunt, she was sure, would never travel any more. She had said only that very morning, that once she got back to England she would stay there for the rest of her life, she was too old to move about any more.

"'And I,' added Charlotte, with a fresh burst of weeping, 'I am to be sent to an English school as soon as aunt can settle about it.'

"'But you will be happier at school, dear,' said Mademoiselle Eliane. 'You will have friends of your own age.'

"'I don't want friends of my own age. I shall never love *any* friends as much as my dear Mademoiselle Jeanne and my dear Mademoiselle Eliane,' sobbed Charlotte; and the only thing that consoled her at all was when the two young ladies found for her among their little treasures a very prettily painted 'bonbonnière,' and a quaint little workcase, fitted with thimble, scissors, and all such things, which she promised them she would always keep, *always*, as souvenirs of their kindness.

"And in return, the poor little thing went out with her aunt's maid the next morning and bought two little keepsakes—a scent-bottle for Mademoiselle Jeanne, and a fan for Mademoiselle Eliane. She spent on them all the money she had; and at this very moment," added Dudu, "the scent-bottle is downstairs in your mother's large old dressing-case, the dressing-case she got from her grandfather. What became of the fan I cannot say.

"Well, the few remaining days passed, and one cold, dreary morning poor Charlotte clambered over the railings for the last time, to embrace her friends and bid them farewell. She might have come in by the door and seen them in the salon; of course neither her aunt nor our young ladies' mother would have objected to such a thing, as she was going away, even though no visits of ceremony had been exchanged between the families. But this would not have suited Charlotte; it was in the garden she had first seen her friends, and in the garden must she bid them good-bye. I assisted at the interview," continued Dudu, "and very touching it was. Had I been of a nature to shed tears, I really think my feelings would have been too much for me. And Charlotte would have kissed and hugged me too, no doubt, had I encouraged anything of the kind. But, fortunately perhaps for the preservation of my feathers and my dignity, I am not, and never have been, of a demonstrative disposition."

Dudu cleared his throat and stopped to rest for a moment. Then he continued—

"The parting was over at last, and little Charlotte was away—quite away over the sea in cold, rainy England. Cold and rainy it must have been that winter in any case, for it was cold and rainy even here, and many changes happened, and shadows of strange events were already faintly darkening the future. It was the next year that our pretty Mademoiselle Jeanne married and went away with her husband from the old house, which yet was to be her home, and the home of her children in the end, for Mademoiselle Eliane never married, and so all came to be inherited by her sister's sons. But with that we have nothing to do at present. I wished only to tell you what concerns our young ladies' friendship with the little stranger. Years went on, as they always do, whether they leave the world happy or miserable, and the shadows I have told you of grew darker and darker. Then, at last, the terrible days began—the storm burst forth, our happy, peaceful home, with hundreds and thousands of others, was broken up, and its kindly inhabitants forced to flee. Mademoiselle Jeanne came hurrying up from her husband's home, where things were even worse than with us, with her boys, to seek for shelter and safety, which, alas! could not be given her here. For all had to flee—my poor old master, frail as he was, his delicate wife, our young ladies, and the boys—all fled together, and after facing perils such as I trust none of their descendants will ever know, they reached a safe refuge. And then they had to endure a new misery, for months and months went by before they had any tidings of poor Mademoiselle Jeanne's husband, your great-grandfather, my children, who, like all of his name—a name you may well be proud of, my little Mademoiselle Jeanne—stayed at the post of danger till every hope was passed. Then at last, in disguise, he managed to escape, and reached this place in safety, hoping here to find something to guide him as to where his wife and children were. But he found nothing—the house was deserted, not a servant or retainer of any kind left except myself, and what, alas! could *I* do? He was worn out and exhausted, poor man; he hid in the house for a few days, creeping out at dusk in fear and trembling to buy a loaf of bread, trusting to his disguise and to his not being well known in the town. But he would have died, I believe, had he been long left as he was, for distress of mind added to his other miseries, not knowing anything as to what had become of your great-grandmother and his children.

"She was a good wife," continued Dudu, after another little pause. "Our Mademoiselle Jeanne, I mean. Just when her poor husband was losing heart altogether, beginning to think they must all be dead, that there was nothing left for him to do but to die too, she came to him. She had travelled alone, quite alone, our delicate young lady—who in former days had scarcely been allowed to set her little foot on the pavement—from Switzerland to the old home, with a strange belief that here if anywhere she should find him. And she was rewarded. The worst of the terrible days were now past, but still disguise was necessary, and it was in the dress of one of her own peasants—the dress in which she had fled—that Mademoiselle Jeanne returned. But he knew her —through all disguises he would have known her —and she him. And the first evening they were together in the bare, deserted house, even with all the terrors behind them, the perils before them, the husband and wife were happy."

Dudu paused again. The children, too interested to speak, listened eagerly.

"Go on, dear Dudu," whispered Jeanne at last, softly.

"How were they to get away to safety? That was the question," continued Dudu. "They dared not stay long where they were; yet they dared not go. Monsieur was far too feeble to stand much fatigue, and the two of them journeying together might attract notice.

"'If we could get to the sea,' said Mademoiselle Jeanne—Madame I should call her, but it never comes naturally — there we might find a ship to take us to England or Holland, and thence find our way to our dear ones again.'

"But Monsieur shook his head. 'Impossible,' he said. 'I have not the strength for even the four leagues' walk to the sea, and finding a ship that would take us is a mere chance. We have almost no money. Here at least we have shelter, and still some sous for bread. Jeanne, my beloved, you must make up your mind to leave me again—alone and unhindered you might find your way back in safety.'

"'I will never leave you,' said Jeanne. 'We will die together, if it must be so. The boys are safe—my father and mother and Eliane will care for them. I will never leave you.'

"And Monsieur said no more; but in his own mind I could see that he thought himself fast dying, that want of comforts and nourishment much longer would exhaust his little strength, and that his poor Jeanne would, in the end, be forced to attempt the journey back alone. They were sitting at the end of the terrace walk that evening—the end near little Charlotte's balcony; it was a mild, still evening—it seemed less dreary and miserable than in the house; from the distance came the sound of the children playing in the old streets, and near at hand some birds were singing still—for children will play and birds will sing whatever happens. Suddenly a sound close at hand made Mademoiselle Jeanne look up. And I too, for I was close beside them on the terrace, I looked up in amazement, half imagining it must be a dream. For we heard—both Mademoiselle Jeanne and I knew it again—the sound of the window on to the balcony opening, the window through which the little English girl used to come out to meet her friends. We looked and could scarcely believe our eyes. Out on to the balcony stepped a young lady, a young girl rather she seemed, for she was tall and slight and had fair curls about her sweet fresh face. She stood for one instant looking at us all as if bewildered, then, with a sudden cry, almost before we knew what she was doing, she was over the railings and down the bank.

"'Mademoiselle Jeanne or Mademoiselle Eliane!' she cried, 'which of you is it? for it is one of you, I know! And you are *not* dead—not all dead and gone—and there is Dudu, too. Oh, how glad, how very glad, I am that I came!'

"Laughing and crying both at once, she threw herself into Madame's arms, while Monsieur looked on in amazement.

"'You know me?' she cried—'your little English Charlotte. See, here is the bonbonnière,' feeling for it in her pocket as she spoke. 'And you are Mademoiselle Jeanne. I know you now—if you had twenty peasant caps on I should know you. But how thin and pale you are, my poor Jeanne!

And is this your husband? I knew you were married. I saw it in the newspapers ever so many years ago. Do you know it is fifteen years since I went away? And I am married, too. But tell me first how it is you are here and dressed like that, and why you look so sad and Monsieur so ill. Tell me all. You may trust me, you may indeed, and perhaps my husband and I may be able to be of some use. You may trust me,' seeing that Madame and her husband looked at each other in bewilderment; 'may they not, Dudu?' she added, turning to me. 'Tell Mademoiselle Jeanne that she can indeed trust me.'

"I flapped my wings and croaked.

"'You see,' said Charlotte, and at that they all laughed.

"'It is not that we do not trust you, my dear friend,' said Madame; 'and indeed you see all in seeing us here as you do. There is nothing to tell but the same sad story that has been to tell in so many once happy French homes. But explain to me, my dear Charlotte, how you are here. It is so strange, so extraordinary.'

And Charlotte explained. Her husband was a sailor. To be near him, she had been in Spain at the outbreak of the revolution, and had remained there till he was ordered home. Now that the terror was subsiding, there was—for them, as foreigners—but little risk. She had persuaded her husband, whose vessel, owing to some slight accident at sea, had been obliged to put in at the neighbouring port, to let her come to have a look at the old town, at the old house, or garden rather, she still loved so dearly. 'The house we used to live in,' she said, 'was empty. I easily found my way in, and out on to the balcony, as you saw. I had a sort of wild idea that perhaps I might see or hear something of you. Yet I was almost afraid to ask, such terrible things have happened,' added Charlotte, with a shudder.

"But nothing more terrible was in store for our young ladies, I am glad to say," continued Dudu. "The faithful-hearted Charlotte and her husband were able to be of the greatest service to Mademoiselle Jeanne and *her* husband. They conveyed them in safety to the port and saw them on board a friendly vessel, and not many weeks passed before they were again with their children and the old Monsieur and Madame and Mademoiselle Eliane in their home for the time in Switzerland."

"Oh, how glad I am!" exclaimed Jeanne. "I was

dreadfully afraid your story was going to end badly, Dudu."

"It is not ended yet," said Dudu.

"Isn't it?" cried Jeanne. "Oh dear, then go on quick, please. I *hope* Mademoiselle Jeanne's poor husband——"

"Your great-grandfather, you mean," corrected Dudu.

"Oh, well then, my great-grandfather, *our* great-grandfather, for he was Chéri's, too, you said. I do so hope he got better. Did he, Dudu?"

"Yes," said Dudu, "he got better, but never quite well again. However, he lived some years, long enough to see his boys grown up and to return—after the death of our old Monsieur and Madame—to return to his own country with his wife and sister-in-law. But before very long, while still far from an old man, he died. Then our young ladies, young no longer, came back, after a time, to their childish home; and here they lived together quietly, kind and charitable to all, cheered from time to time by the visits of Madame's two sons, out in the world now and married, and with homes of their own. And time went on gently and uneventfully, and gradually Madame's hair became quite, quite white, and Mademoiselle

Eliane took to limping a little in her walk with the rheumatism, and when they slowly paced up and down the terrace it was difficult for me to think they were really my pretty young ladies with the white dresses and blue ribbons of half a century ago. For it was now just thirty-five years since the last visit of their English friend. She too, if she were alive, must be a woman of more than sixty. They had never heard of her again. In the hurry and anxiety of their last meeting they had forgotten to ask and she to give her exact address, so they could not write. She might have written to them to the old house perhaps, on the chance of it finding them; but if so, they had never got the letter. Yet they often spoke of her, and never saw the balcony at the end of the terrace without a kindly thought of those long ago days.

"One evening—an autumn evening—mild and balmy, the two old ladies were slowly pacing up and down their favourite walk, when a servant came out to say that they were wanted—a lady was asking for them. But not to disturb them, he added, the visitor would be glad to see them in the garden, if they would allow it. Wondering who it could be, Madame and her sister were hesitating what to do, when a figure was seen approaching them from the house.

"'I could not wait,' she said, almost before she reached them. 'I wished so much to see you once more in the old spot, dear friends;' and they knew her at once. They recognised in the bowed and worn but still sweet and lovely woman, their pretty child-friend of fifty years ago. She had come to bid them farewell, she said. She was on her way to the south—not to live but to die, for she had suffered much and her days were numbered.

"'My dear husband is dead some years ago,' she said. 'But we were very happy together, which is a blessed thought. And my children—one after another they faded. So I am an old woman now and quite alone, and I am glad to go to them all. My friends wished me to go to the south, for I have always loved the sunshine, and there my little daughter died, and perhaps death will there come to me in gentler shape. But on my way, I wished to say good-bye to you, dear friends of long ago, whom I have always loved, though we have been so little together.'

"And then they took each other's hands, gently and quietly, the three old ladies, and softly kissed each other's withered cheeks, down which a few tears made their way; the time was past for them for anything but gentle and chastened feelings. And whispering to their old friend not good-bye, but 'Au revoir, au revoir in a better country,' my ladies parted once more with their childish friend.

"She died a few months later; news of her death was sent them. *They* lived to be old—past eighty both of them, when they died within a few days of each other. But I never hobble up and down the terrace walk without thinking of them," added Dudu, "and on the whole, my dears, even if I had my choice, I don't think I should care to live another two or three hundred years in a world where changes come so quickly."

Hugh and Jeanne were silent for a moment. Then "Thank you, dear Dudu," they said together.

And Dudu cocked his head on one side. "There is Marcelline calling you," he said, in a matter-of-fact tone. "Run downstairs. Take a look at the beautiful stars overhead before you go. Good-bye, my dears."

"Good-night, Dudu, and thank you again," said the children, as they hastened away.

They found their way back to the tapestry room without difficulty. They were standing in the middle of the room, half puzzled as to how they had got there, when Marcelline appeared.

"We have been with Dudu," they told her, before she had time to ask them anything. "He has told us lovely stories—nicer even than fairy adventures." And Marcelline smiled and seemed pleased, but not at all surprised.

"A strange thing has happened," said Jeanne's father the next day. "I feel quite distressed about it. Old Dudu the raven has disappeared. He is nowhere to be found since yesterday afternoon, the gardener tells me. They have looked for him everywhere in vain. I feel quite sorry—he has been in the family so long—how long indeed I should be afraid to say, for my father remembered him as a child."

The children looked at each other.

"Dudu has gone!" they said softly.

"We shall have no more stories," whispered Hugh.

"Nor fairy adventures," said Jeanne.

"He may come back again," said Hugh.

"I think not," said Jeanne, shaking her smooth little black head. "Don't you remember, Chéri, what he said about not wishing to stay here longer?"

"And he said 'good-bye,'" added Hugh sadly. "I fear he will not come back."

But if he *ever* does, children dear, and if you care to hear what he has to tell, you shall not be forgotten, I promise you.

THE END

Tom Stacey

BOOKS FOR CHILDREN

To many parents, aunts, uncles, grandparents and great grand-parents these Stacey books for the young will be familiar favourites, but to modern children in England today they will be quite new:

THE MERRY ADVENTURES OF ROBIN HOOD

written and illustrated by Howard Pyle **£2.25**

A timeless classic—not just for children or just for adults, but for everyone with imagination and an open heart. Here are all the good old stories, dressed up fresh in Lincoln Green. Here are merry Robin, a certain stout fellow called Little John, Friar Tuck, Allan-a-Dale and all the rest of that famous company. Sober-sided persons who think that history should be a solemn affair and that facts are more important than legends had better pass on quickly. This book is not for them.

RACKETTY-PACKETTY HOUSE

by Frances Hodgson Burnett; illustrated by Harrison Cady **£1.30**

This is a story about two families of dolls—the humble and happy family which lived in Racketty-Packetty House and the proud, bad-tempered family which lived in Tidy Castle—and about what happened to them when no-one was looking. It is one of Frances Hodgson Burnett's most delightful books for small children.

THE COZY LION

by Frances Hodgson Burnett; illustrated by Harrison Cady **£1.30**

A companion volume to Racketty-Packetty House, it is the story of a rather naughty lion, who was fond of terrorising the village and eating people, but who really wanted to be loved and played with by the children. It tells how the fairy, Queen Crosspatch, finally succeeds in reforming him and in teaching him how to be a very gentle, cozy lion indeed.

OLD MOTHER WEST WIND and its companion volume
MOTHER WEST WIND'S CHILDREN

by Thornton W. Burgess; illustrated by Harrison Cady **£1.70 each**

"Old Mother West Wind came down from the Purple Hills in the golden light of the early morning. Over her shoulders was slung a bag—a great big bag—and in the bag were all of Old Mother West Wind's Children . . ."
Long ago, children began to read and listen to the book with this wonderful opening and to the stories about the little people of the Green Forest and the Green Meadows: Peter Rabbit, Hooty the Owl, Reddy Fox and their companions. Now here they are again with new colour illustrations by Harrison Cady—the best of all bedtime stories for children.

THE PELICAN AND THE KANGAROO

by Eric M. Silvanus; illustrated by P. B. Longson **£1.80**

This is a story of long ago and far away. It is the story of a beautiful kangaroo Princess called Euphemia, and of the pelican Prince Dauphin, who found her sailing all alone on the empty ocean. It tells how they fell in love; and how they went in search of the oldest jewel in the world. It is a story of

Magic and Mystery
Nonsense and History

It is irresistible.

THE HIRED MAN'S ELEPHANT

by Phil Stong; illustrated by Doris Lee **£1.40**

This prize-winning children's book by the author of that evergreen American classic, *State Fair,* is now published in Britain for the first time. It describes how a very well behaved performing elephant called Ali comes to town with his master and mistress, makes a great many friends, and—temporarily—at least one enemy, and surprises the local mayor and policeman into doing the most unexpected things.

THE TAPESTRY ROOM

by Mrs Molesworth with Walter Crane's original illustrations **£1.50**

Marghanita Laski said of this book:

> "Here Mrs Molesworth successfully combines all the ingredients for the enchantment of children."

The sure and simple touch of the famous Victorian children's author is as fresh today as when this marvellous book was written. The characters Jeanne and Hugh may belong to another age, but their love of fairy stories, their dreams and delights and fears, belong to any small child at any time.

THE UGLY DACHSHUND

by G. B. Stern; illustrated by K. F. Barker **£1.20**

Tono could never understand why his dinner was chunks of raw meat, when the other dachshunds were given carefully cooked and mashed-up dinners. And he felt as jealous as his good nature would allow him to be when little Erda was taken up into the crook of her master's arm while he was left to walk on his own. The answer to these puzzles never occurred to the patient, gentle and very faithful dog who believed himself to be a dachshund, until one bright summer morning when he saw himself for what he was—a Great Dane.

The Ugly Dachshund owes its inspiration to Hans Christian Andersen, but children and adults alike will appreciate its own very individual humour and charm.

THE CARVED CARTOON

by Austin Clare **£1.80**

Grinling Gibbons, the great wood carver whose work is one of England's treasures, is a shadowy figure. But here Austin Clare has pieced together his story in an adventure as exciting as that of any famous hero, as full of action and passion as any romance. In the fascinating but dangerous London of Charles II, against a background which includes the Great Plague and the Great Fire, Grinling Gibbons must endure many perils and hardships until he emerges triumphant to join Sir Christopher Wren in the rebuilding of St Paul's Cathedral.

MASTER SKYLARK

by John Bennett **£1.80**

In this book, which has been remembered and loved though out of print for many years, John Bennett beautifully recreates that springtime of England's glory, the years of Queen Bess and Will Shakespeare, with all the excitement and emotion, the hopes and terrors, the affection and the laughter and the tears of real people—people like young Nick Attwood who finds himself tricked into joining a players' company and carried off with them to London and an unknown future.

Tom Stacey Ltd

28-29 Maiden Lane, London WC2E 7JP